CAREC TRANSPORT STRATEGY 2030

JANUARY 2020

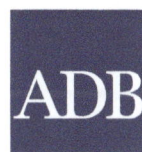

© 2020 Asian Development Bank
6 ADB Avenue, Mandaluyong City, 1550 Metro Manila, Philippines
Tel +63 2 8632 4444; Fax +63 2 8636 2444
www.adb.org

Some rights reserved. Published in 2020.

ISBN 978-92-9261-999-2 (print), 978-92-9262-000-4 (electronic), 978-92-9262-001-1 (ebook)
Publication Stock No. SPR200024-2
DOI: http://dx.doi.org/10.22617/SPR200024-2

The views expressed in this publication are those of the authors and do not necessarily reflect the views and policies of the Asian Development Bank (ADB) or its Board of Governors or the governments they represent.

ADB does not guarantee the accuracy of the data included in this publication and accepts no responsibility for any consequence of their use. The mention of specific companies or products of manufacturers does not imply that they are endorsed or recommended by ADB in preference to others of a similar nature that are not mentioned.

By making any designation of or reference to a particular territory or geographic area, or by using the term "country" in this document, ADB does not intend to make any judgments as to the legal or other status of any territory or area.

Please contact pubsmarketing@adb.org if you have questions or comments with respect to content, or if you wish to obtain copyright permission for your intended use that does not fall within these terms, or for permission to use the ADB logo.

Corrigenda to ADB publications may be found at http://www.adb.org/publications/corrigenda.

Notes:
In this publication, "$" refers to US dollars.
ADB recognizes "China" as the People's Republic of China.

Contents

Tables, Figures, Box, and Maps

TABLES

FIGURES

BOX

MAPS

Abbreviations

ADB	–	Asian Development Bank
CAREC	–	Central Asia Regional Economic Cooperation
CBTLF	–	cross-border transport and logistics facilitation
CFCFA	–	CAREC Federation of Carrier and Forwarders Association
CPMM	–	Corridor Performance Measurement and Monitoring
CTS	–	CAREC Transport Strategy
DMC	–	developing member country
ICT	–	information and communication technology
km	–	kilometer
km/ hr	–	kilometer/hour
PBM	–	performance-based maintenance
PRC	–	People's Republic of China
PPP	–	public–private partnership
RAMS	–	Road Asset Management System
SWD	–	speed with delay
SWOD	–	speed without delay
TSCC	–	Transport Sector Coordinating Committee
TSPR	–	Transport Sector Progress Report
TTFS	–	Transport and Trade Facilitation Strategy

Executive Summary

The new Central Asia Regional Economic Cooperation (CAREC) Transport Strategy 2030 builds on progress made and lessons learned from the CAREC Transport and Trade Facilitation Strategy 2020. It links to the overall CAREC 2030 program in the areas of enhanced connectivity and sustainability. In this strategy, trade facilitation has been separated from transport. The Transport Strategy will be implemented in conjunction with the CAREC Integrated Trade Agenda 2030. Each is now more strongly aligned to CAREC 2030 goals. Under the 2020 strategy, goals of 7,800 kilometers (km) of CAREC corridor roads and 1,800 km of rail track built were achieved by 2017. However, under 2030, the strategy will emphasize increasing sustainability and network quality, in addition to construction and rehabilitation of transport corridors. Going forward, more emphasis will be placed on multimodal connectivity, road asset management, road safety, and performance-based maintenance goals. Knowledge work in these areas will be actively translated into policy actions in the CAREC countries through demand-based approaches.

Reporting, through annual CAREC Transport Reports, will be more disaggregated than before. Previously, the secretariat tended to report averages, which masked the tremendous variation in the region. Disaggregation and provision of specific examples will make it easier for a developing member country (DMC) to analyze its own network against others' networks, providing useful data to positively influence national planning, cooperation, and peer-to-peer learning. Similarly, future knowledge work will be more flexible and demand driven. Products will be designed as practical decision-support tools for the CAREC DMCs.

The focus of the strategy builds on the five strategic pillars of roads and road asset management, railways, cross-border transport and logistics, road safety, and aviation as their relevance to the CAREC DMCs has been confirmed; however, it is also open to the inclusion of new strategic transport pillars in response to emerging priorities of the CAREC DMCs and development partners. Performance of cross-border transport and logistics has been identified as a particularly weak point of the program to date. Therefore, the strategy commits to strengthen its focus on building trust and cooperation among the CAREC DMCs to reduce nonphysical trade and logistics barriers. Particular attention and support will be given to those countries where procedural and infrastructure bottlenecks are high, negatively impacting the overall performance of individual corridors and the entire network. The strategy will also give increasing attention to sea ports, maritime operations, and smooth interoperability between different modes of transport to establish seamless multimodal corridors within the CAREC region and with the rest of the world.

The new strategy builds upon its predecessor, offering CAREC as a vehicle to help facilitate more innovative financing for increasingly large or complex projects of regional importance. This includes road and rail corridors that enhance the CAREC mission to establish a regional cooperation platform to connect people, policies, and projects for shared and sustainable development. Such financing strategies will include avenues for private sector participation and will build upon initiatives, such as pilot initiatives, which successfully foster collaboration among private freight operators along CAREC corridors, multidonor steering groups for regional rail corridors, and the development of revenue-generation models for proposed megaprojects, such as the Second Salang Tunnel on Corridors 5 and 6.

The CAREC program will continue to provide a communication and coordination platform for the CAREC DMCs and development partners to present and discuss new projects and transport initiatives. This will enable DMCs to align their priorities with each other and build a well-connected transport network, regulations, and operational practices. The strategy will support the CAREC sustainability agenda by addressing the strong demand to convert transport infrastructure investments into sustainable economic and social development for the region.

CHAPTER I

Introduction

1.   The Central Asia Regional Economic Cooperation (CAREC) program is a partnership of 11 developing member countries (DMCs)[1] and development partners working together to promote development through cooperation, to drive accelerated economic growth and poverty reduction. It is guided by the overarching vision of "Good Neighbors, Good Partners, and Good Prospects." The program covers several operational clusters, including Economic and Infrastructure Connectivity which includes the Transport and Energy sectors.

2.   At the 16th CAREC Ministerial Conference in 2017, the ministers endorsed *CAREC 2030: Connecting the Region for Shared and Sustainable Development (CAREC 2030)*, the new strategic framework that will guide the program through to 2030. CAREC 2030 builds on the solid foundation of progress made under CAREC 2020, while updating its strategic directions to respond more effectively to the region's long-term development challenges. CAREC 2030 is inspired by a mission to create an open and inclusive regional cooperation platform that connects people, policies, and projects for shared and sustainable development.

3.   Following endorsement of the new CAREC 2030 framework, a new CAREC Integrated Trade Agenda 2030 was prepared and endorsed in November 2018; and then this CAREC Transport Strategy (CTS) 2030 was prepared and endorsed by the CAREC Ministers in November 2019. Development of separate strategic plans for trade and transport should not be viewed as fragmentation of the trade and transport agenda, but rather as a deeper response to a call for stronger alignment of all CAREC operational clusters toward achieving CAREC 2030 goals for connecting the region for shared sustainable economic and social development.

4.   In recognition of the strong linkages between transport and trade, the new CTS 2030 is fully aligned with the objectives of reducing trade barriers and costs, increasing trade connectivity, and reducing trade turnover times. At the same time, it looks more at the sustainability of transport systems. Within the scope of the CAREC Transport and Trade Facilitation Strategy (TTFS) 2020, progress was made in setting the strategic direction for the railway sector through Unlocking Potential of Railways: A Railway Strategy of CAREC, 2017–2030[2] and road safety management through Safely Connected: A Regional Road Safety Strategy for CAREC Countries, 2017–2030.[3] Working groups were established, capacity development seminars were held, and knowledge products were produced and disseminated in five key pillars of the CAREC Transport Sector: (i) cross-border transport and logistics, (ii) roads and road asset management, (iii) road safety management, (iv) railways, and (v) aviation. The CTS 2030 builds on these five key pillars, but is flexible to be able to adapt to changing priorities of the CAREC DMCs and development partners.

---

[1]   Afghanistan, Azerbaijan, Georgia, Kazakhstan, Kyrgyz Republic, Mongolia, Pakistan, People's Republic of China, Tajikistan, Turkmenistan, and Uzbekistan.

[2]   Asian Development Bank (ADB). 2017. *Unblocking the Potential of Railways: A Railway Strategy for CAREC (2017–2030)*. Manila. https://www.adb.org/documents/railway-strategy-carec-2017-2030.

[3]   ADB. 2017. *Safely Connected: A Regional Road Safety Strategy for CAREC Countries (2017–2030)*. Manila. https://www.adb.org/documents/road-safety-strategy-carec-2017-2030.

CHAPTER II

Lessons Learned

5.   Most CAREC counties are landlocked, but have relatively good overland connectivity to their main trading partners in Europe, East Asia, and Middle Asia. Over the last decade, some CAREC DMCs successfully established transport land bridges between the fast-growing East Asia and Western Europe. The CAREC TTFS 2020 targets to build 7,800 kilometers (km) of roads and 1,800 km of rail track by 2020 were both exceeded by 2017. The road and rail infrastructure investments centered along the six CAREC transport corridors, and all major CAREC projects were within the CAREC geographic area.

6.   Map 1 illustrates the six CAREC multimodal corridors which continue to guide transport infrastructure development in the new transport strategy. Corridors 1, 3, 4, 5, and 6 remain as defined in the TTFS 2020 (Appendix 1). Corridor 2 was revised in 2017 after Georgia joined the CAREC program. The corridor extension to Georgia expands the CAREC multimodal network connectivity to the Black Sea ports and the land border with Turkey.

7.   Going forward, CAREC member countries will continue to prioritize investment projects and transport initiatives along CAREC corridors, with greater emphasis on multimodal connectivity, road asset management, and road safety. Within the framework of the new transport strategy, the six corridors are viewed as a network of economic connectivity. The CAREC corridor network includes branch roads and railways and logistics facilities, in addition to the main CAREC highways and railways.

8.   Despite the strong progress in infrastructure development outputs, the key outcomes of the TTFS 2020, such as improvement in average speed and reduction in cost of travel along the CAREC corridors, did not improve. In 2018, the average speed of travel along all six CAREC corridors reached 21.3 kilometers per hour (km/h), which falls short of the 2020 target of 30 km/h and is below the 2010 baseline of 23.5 km/h. Nevertheless, the average number does not show the entire picture. The average speed performance of each of the six CAREC corridors differs significantly, ranging for road transport from 6 km/h in Corridor 6d to 34 km/h in Corridor 1a.[4]

9.   Moreover, progress with infrastructure development does not always translate directly to improved trade and transport-related outcomes. Therefore, the CAREC program will further strengthen its focus on increasing mutual trust and cooperation among CAREC member countries to reduce nonphysical trade and logistics barriers. More knowledge dissemination activities and capacity development support will be provided to all countries which seek to improve cross-border transport and logistics. Particular attention and support will be given to countries where procedural and infrastructure bottlenecks are high and the performance of individual corridors and the entire network is impacted.

10.   To understand performance of individual countries and CAREC corridors requires disaggregated performance monitoring.

---

[4]   ADB. 2019. *CAREC Corridor Performance Measurement and Monitoring Annual Report 2018.* Manila. https://www.adb.org/publications/carec-cpmm-annual-report-2018.

Map 1: CAREC Multimodal Corridors

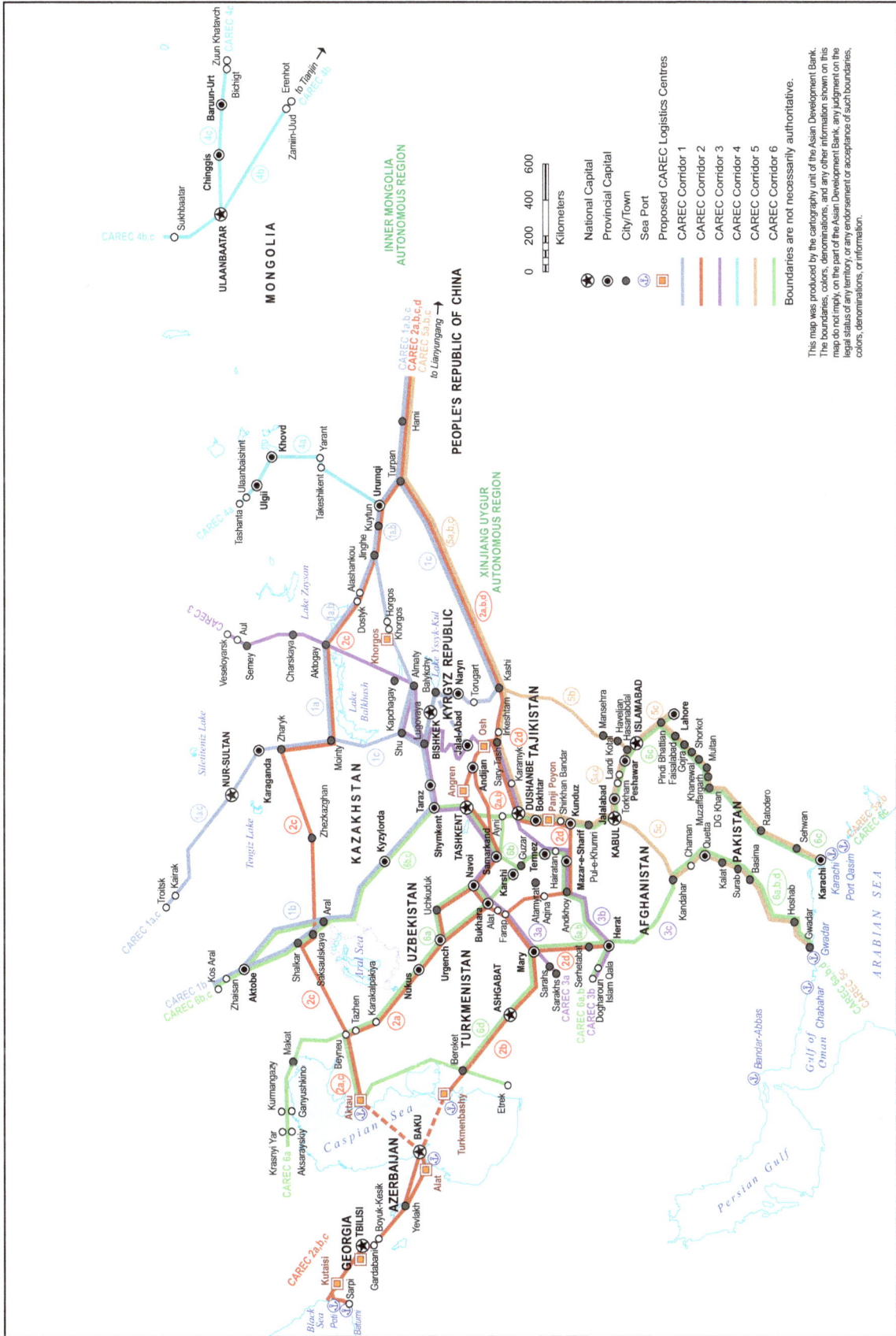

MONGOLIA

INNER MONGOLIA AUTONOMOUS REGION

PEOPLE'S REPUBLIC OF CHINA

XINJIANG UYGUR AUTONOMOUS REGION

KAZAKHSTAN

KYRGYZ REPUBLIC

UZBEKISTAN

TAJIKISTAN

TURKMENISTAN

AFGHANISTAN

PAKISTAN

GEORGIA

AZERBAIJAN

Caspian Sea

Black Sea

Aral Sea

Lake Balkhash

Lake Zaysan

Tengiz Lake

Silicteniz Lake

Issyk-Kul

ARABIAN SEA

Persian Gulf

Gulf of Oman

National Capital
Provincial Capital
City/Town
Sea Port
Proposed CAREC Logistics Centres
CAREC Corridor 1
CAREC Corridor 2
CAREC Corridor 3
CAREC Corridor 4
CAREC Corridor 5
CAREC Corridor 6

Boundaries are not necessarily authoritative.

0   200   400   600
Kilometers

This map was produced by the cartography unit of the Asian Development Bank. The boundaries, colors, denominations, and any other information shown on this map do not imply, on the part of the Asian Development Bank, any judgment on the legal status of any territory, or any endorsement or acceptance of such boundaries, colors, denominations, or information.

cars 19-1648 AV

Source: CAREC Secretariat.

Reporting for the CAREC program will shift from average performance indicators to disaggregated performance indicators. A set of comprehensive indicators and analytical reports disaggregated by individual countries and corridors will be developed. This will provide useful reference information, comparative analysis, and recommendations for consideration and decision making to the relevant government authorities of the CAREC DMCs.

11.   The CAREC Corridor Performance Measurement and Monitoring (CPMM), launched in 2010, meets these requirements and will continue to be the primary source of information for transport operations and challenges along the CAREC corridors. Data collected under the CPMM to date will be used to develop analytical reports to support the CAREC DMCs in their efforts to improve infrastructure of the CAREC corridors and related procedures.

12.   The CAREC Transport Sector Progress Report (TSPR) will continue to provide annual progress updates across the key pillars of the CAREC Transport Sector's work. The TSPR will give an opportunity to all the CAREC DMCs to share progress updates with each other regarding their priority transport investment projects, priority investment plans, and needs over the next several years. The TSPR will also provide linked, in-depth reports on particular transport sector topics of interest, such as achievements in road safety, railways, road asset management, or other topics of interest.

13.   CAREC will encourage private sector participation in the funding and operation of transport assets, as a mechanism to boost efficiency, widen the funding base, improve risk management, and encourage institutional reform of state-owned transport operators. The CAREC Federation of Carrier and Forwarder Associations (CFCFA) has successfully piloted collaboration initiatives between private freight operators along CAREC corridors and will expand the pilots and implement other joint public–private initiatives as part of the CTS 2030.

CHAPTER III

CAREC Transport Sector Strategic Framework

14.   The CAREC Transport Sector's priorities are fully aligned with the CAREC mission to establish a *regional cooperation platform to connect people, policies, and projects for shared and sustainable development.* The key objectives of the CAREC Transport Strategy are *connectivity and sustainability*.

15.   For improved trade and transport *connectivity*, the CAREC DMCs and development partners will focus on prioritizing and implementing transport infrastructure development projects along the CAREC corridors (refer to Appendix 2 for the list of priority projects). The CAREC program will provide a communication and coordination platform for the CAREC DMCs and development partners to present and discuss new projects and transport initiatives. The platform will continue to support DMCs in aligning their priorities, building a well-connected transport network, and improving regulation and operation practices. Through the CAREC program, individual DMCs will be able to consolidate support for initiatives among their neighbors and raise development financing jointly for the implementation of large-scale infrastructure projects.

16.   During the CTS 2030 implementation period, the CAREC DMCs and development partners will increase their attention to operational procedures and equipment harmonization to enable smooth multimodal operations along the CAREC corridors. Ports and shipping operations

will be better aligned with land transport through deployment of modern information and communication technology (ICT), harmonized shipping data standards, transport documents, scheduling of operations, and institutional reforms. Private transport and logistics operators will be engaged to diagnose connectivity issues and identify priorities for cross-border multimodal transport and logistics improvements to better align cross-border transport operations in CAREC countries.

17.   The CAREC program will continue promoting best practice quality standards in transport project design and implementation. Robust safeguards and environmental standards, high quality and sustainable design, transparent procurement, and efficient project implementation practices are trademarks of the CAREC program. As much as possible, infrastructure development projects will incorporate sustainable development elements, including greener transport, which will further enhance their regional economic and social impact.

18.   The *sustainability* agenda will receive maximum attention given the strong demand to convert transport infrastructure investments into sustainable economic and social development. Particular attention will be given to reducing cross-border trade and logistics barriers to support the growth of free trade and economic development within the CAREC region. The importance of improved financing and management of road and railway assets for more sustainable transport

infrastructure investment will be a key focus of CAREC knowledge products and institutional capacity development activities. Contemporary road safety principles and practices will be further integrated into transport infrastructure and operations through consistent implementation of priority actions under the CAREC Road Safety Strategy 2030.

19.   Under the CTS 2030, activities under each of the key pillars of the CAREC Transport Sector are expected to contribute to both increased regional connectivity and greater sustainability of the regional transport system (Table 1).

Table 1: CAREC Transport Strategic Framework–Two Objectives and Five Pillars

Transport Pillar	*Connectivity* Objective	*Sustainability* Objective
Cross-Border Transport and Logistics	• Implementation of transport facilitation agreements and conventions and fostering regional transportation dialogue • Improvement of border crossing facilities and procedures • Development of ports and logistics centers facilities and operations to support seamless interoperability of all modes of transport	• Reduced cost of trade, increased trade, and economic growth • Increased efficiency and integrity of public institutions • Improved safety and security
Roads and Road Asset Management	• Sufficient allocation of funds for construction, rehabilitation, and maintenance of roads • Strategic long-term planning for development of the regional and national transport networks to meet growing social, economic, and trade connectivity needs	• Improved economic and social conditions through better connectivity • Strong focus on life-cycle costing and quality for more sustainable infrastructure investments • Financing allocation based on robust analytical and decision support tools, such as the Road Asset Management System (RAMS) • Institutional and procedural reforms for improved national road asset management • Increased private sector participation in road operation and maintenance
Road Safety	• Improved propensity to travel due to increased safety	• Increased road safety leading to reduced life and health impacts, and economic losses.
Railways	• Construction, rehabilitation, modernization and maintenance of railroads • Development of stations and intermodal facilities • Purchase and maintenance of rolling stock suited to emerging needs • Effective commercial and efficient operational practices • Digitalization of railways to improve operational coordination and to support management decision making	• Improved economic and social conditions through reduced service cost and improved quality of service • Sustainable operational practices, inclusive financial and life-cycle cost management, railways assets management and upgrade, staff qualifications • Enhanced safety and security for all users, especially women • Improved environmental sustainability through modal shift, energy efficiency improvements, and fuel switch
Aviation	• Development of airports and public transport linkages • Regional and national policies and agreements to foster open markets competition and cooperation • Improved efficiency of air freight	• Increased economic opportunities through trade, industry, and tourism • Increased efficiency, safety, and security • Improved economic and social conditions through reduced service cost and improved quality of service

Source: CAREC Secretariat.

CHAPTER IV

Strategic Pillar—Cross-Border Transport and Logistics Facilitation

20. **CAREC and Cross-Border Transport and Logistics Facilitation (CBTLF).** From its very inception, the CAREC program focused on improving cross-border movement of people and cargo. The CAREC program developed a holistic approach toward trade and transport facilitation, reflected in the philosophy of the CAREC Transport and Trade Facilitation Strategy (CAREC TTFS). The CAREC TTFS[5] suggested actions for the improvement of customs and other border control procedures; implementation of modern risk management principles in border control of cargo, vehicles, and drivers; improvement of the border crossing infrastructure and equipment; facilitation of cross-border and transit traffic through international transport conventions and agreements, and regional traffic rights agreements; and support in establishing multimodal logistics centers in strategic locations along the CAREC transport corridors.

21. The CAREC TTFS adopted the CAREC corridor-based approach to CBTLF, focusing priority infrastructure investments and transport facilitation actions along six CAREC corridors. The CPMM system was designed to monitor time and costs of road and rail travel across the key border crossing points of the CAREC corridors to understand the impact of CBTLF initiatives. The monitoring started in 2010 and was implemented by the CFCFA. The TTFS also proposed establishing corridor management units for selected pilot corridors and designated railway corridors for more integrated management of the CAREC corridors.

22. **Key issues.** Despite the desire to implement an integrated approach to cross-border transport and logistics, institutional coordination among national transport agencies and border management agencies (BMAs such as customs, border security, sanitary, and phytosanitary) remains weak in most of the CAREC DMCs. Even weaker is the cross-border coordination between BMAs of neighboring countries. As a result, the average time and cost of clearing the border remains very high, and the average speed of travel along CAREC corridors is low (Figure 1). While the average speed of freight traffic by road and rail[6] did not improve over the reporting period of 2010–2018, the speed without delay (SWOD)[7] did show substantial improvement. This suggests that CAREC's actions to improve road and rail infrastructure contributed to increased travel speed, but the gains are lost due to the cumbersome and slow border crossing and other government inspection procedures.

---

[5] CAREC TTFS 2008 and CAREC TTFS 2020.
[6] Speed with delay accounts all stoppages for the government checks and queuing and waiting time.
[7] Speed without delay (SWOD) excludes all stoppages for the government checks and queuing, and accounts only for the productive driving time.

23.   The CAREC CPMM data demonstrated improvements of some border clearance times along selected corridors and at selected border crossing points. In 2018, the best performing border crossing points achieved an average total processing time of 0.1 hours per vehicle for both inbound (import) and outbound (export) traffic, which is in line with the best international standards. At the worst-performing border crossing points, the outbound vehicles experienced an average delay of 65 hours and inbound vehicles experienced an average delay of 25 hours over the 2018 period. Furthermore, the average total processing time reached a staggering 90 hours per vehicle at the worst-performing border crossing point of the CAREC network. The border crossing delays were caused by a variety of factors:

(i)   outdated infrastructure and equipment;
(ii)   poor traffic management during peak seasons and hours resulting in long queues;
(iii) inefficient and duplicative customs, immigration, security, and sanitary and phytosanitary control procedures;
(iv)   absence of effective traffic rights agreements, resulting in transshipment of cargo or long waiting time for special traffic permits;
(v)   absence of effective customs transit guarantee mechanisms, resulting in long waiting times for customs escorts or customs bonds;
(vi)   weak risk management systems and practices; and
(vii) rent seeking by border control officials, resulting in deliberate slowing down of processes for carriers who are not prepared to pay unofficial fees.

24.   The most significant obstacles to free movement of cargo and passengers not captured by CPMM data include absence of traffic rights agreements between selected DMCs, permanent or temporary closures of border crossing points, restrictions on specific types of traffic, bilateral legal status of some CAREC border crossing points, and other restrictive practices. As a result, transit traffic often diverts from the most direct and convenient route and the CPMM did not measure this inefficiency as it only looked at crossing times and not total journey time. Furthermore, these issues may mean transshipment of cargo is required between transport vehicles of neighboring countries, increasing time and cost of transport, and negatively impacting regional trade.

25.   CAREC transport corridors provide overland connectivity to deep-sea ports of the Arabian Sea and Black Sea, providing landlocked countries access to overseas trading partners. Further connectivity improvements can be achieved at the multimodal corridor via the Caspian Sea. Despite significant investments in sea ports and shipping operations, multimodal logistics and transport operations in the region remain slow and costly. Significant delays and additional costs are caused by limited interoperability between water transport and land transport operations, slow border crossing procedures, insufficient logistics facilities, and outdated technology.

26.   **Actions.** In 2015,[8] the CAREC DMCs agreed to adopt principles for freedom of transit within the CAREC geographical area by concluding and fully implementing bilateral and regional cross-border transport agreements (Figure 2) and joining key United Nations Cross-Border Transport Facilitation Agreements and Conventions, including the TIR Convention (1975), Convention on Harmonization of Frontier Control of Goods (1982), and CMR Agreement (1956).[9] By 2017, after accession of Pakistan and the People's Republic of China (PRC), all CAREC member countries were fully covered by

[8]   CAREC 14th Transport Sector Coordinating Committee (TSCC) Meeting. Summary of Proceedings. https://www. carecprogram.org/uploads/2015-TSCC-Summary-Proceedings-14th-CAREC-TSCC2.pdf
[9]   United Nations Economic Commission for Europe. Convention on the Contract for the International Carriage of Goods by Road (CMR), 19 May 1956. https://www.unece.org/fileadmin/DAM/trans/conventn/cmr_e.pdf

Figure 1: Average Speed with Delay and without Delay across Borders along the CAREC Corridors, 2010–2018 (kilometers per hour)

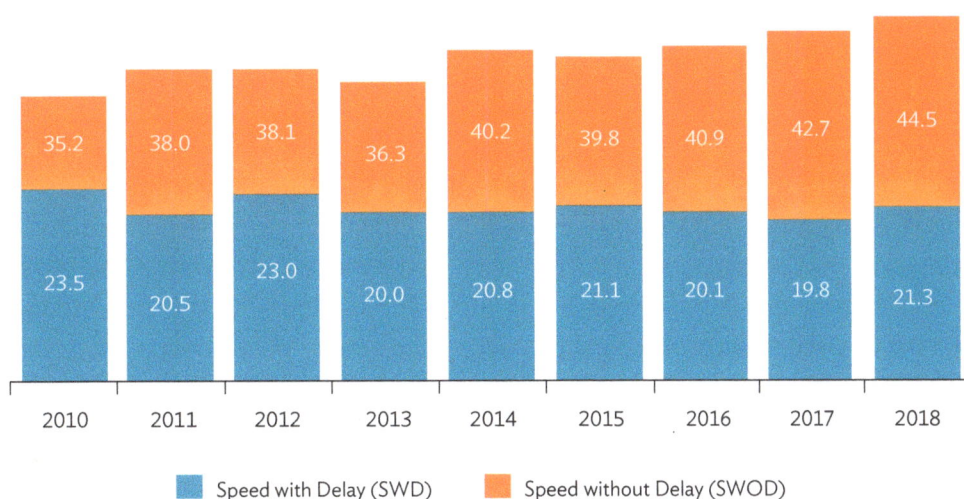

Year	Speed with Delay (SWD)	Speed without Delay (SWOD)
2010	23.5	35.2
2011	20.5	38.0
2012	23.0	38.1
2013	20.0	36.3
2014	20.8	40.2
2015	21.1	39.8
2016	20.1	40.9
2017	19.8	42.7
2018	21.3	44.5

Source: CAREC Secretariat. The Corridor Performance Measurement and Monitoring (CPMM) methodology and data are further explained in *CAREC CPMM Annual Report 2018*.

Figure 2: Components of Bilateral and Regional Cross-Border Transport Agreements

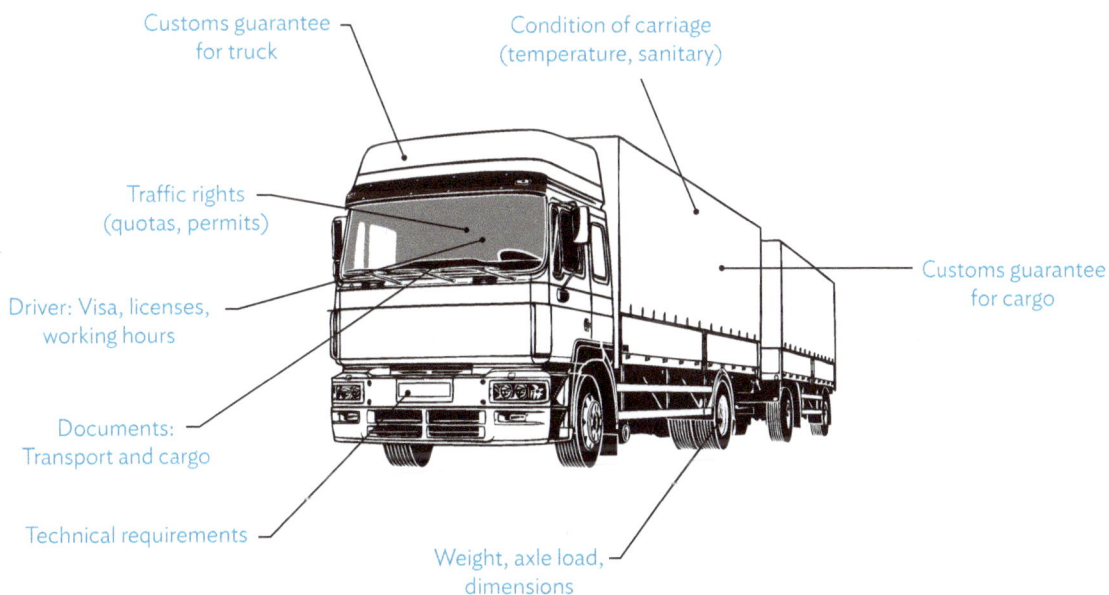

Customs guarantee for truck

Condition of carriage (temperature, sanitary)

Traffic rights (quotas, permits)

Driver: Visa, licenses, working hours

Customs guarantee for cargo

Documents: Transport and cargo

Technical requirements

Weight, axle load, dimensions

Source: CAREC Secretariat. https://www.carecprogram.org/uploads/2015-CBT-Workshop-02-Cross-Border-Transport-Facilitation-in-the-CAREC.pdf.

TIR, with national road transport associations and local chambers of commerce acting as guaranteeing organizations. In parallel with implementation of the TIR customs guarantee mechanism, selected CAREC member countries agreed to pilot the implementation of the CAREC Advanced Transit System, which could in the long run become an alternative CAREC-wide customs transit guarantee mechanism.

27.   Several Regional Improvement of Border Services (RIBS) projects were implemented in CAREC member countries, which implemented a holistic approach to improvement of border crossing points, institutions, and procedures. One substantial component of the RIBS approach was the establishment of integrated management structures for development, maintenance, and coordinated operations of border crossing points. New CAREC projects that follow the RIBS approach will include some of these elements:

(i)   establishment of integrated management structures, such as land port authorities;
(ii)   construction of border crossing point facilities and installation of control equipment;
(iii) deployment of efficient ICT solutions to enable integrated data flow and management;
(iv)   training and capacity development for border management agencies;
(v)   supporting implementation of best practices and legal instruments, such as the Revised Kyoto Convention, WCO Safe Framework, TIR Convention, Harmonization Convention (1982), and others; and
(vi)   supporting implementation of TIR parks and electronic queuing systems to reduce congestion at border crossing points, and reduce unproductive waiting time and exhaust from the queuing vehicles.

28.   A similar integrated approach will be pursued for the development of sea port operations. In April 2019, the CAREC Transport Sector Coordination Committee (TSCC) called for an increase in attention to multimodal operations through regional sea ports. The committee endorsed the preparation of a scoping study to examine key issues and priority actions for the development of seamless multimodal transport and logistics through CAREC seaports. Priority activities examined and recommended within the scoping study included:

(i)   development of knowledge products on ports and shipping, logistics operations and logistics centers to provide support in national policy decision making for specific countries;
(ii)   recommendations for standardization of equipment, operational standards, and schedules to reduce time and cost from poor interoperability. Particular attention was given to increased containerization of freight traffic along the CAREC corridors;
(iii) usage of standardized International Federation of Freight Forwarding Associations (FIATA) freight forwarding documents to be further supported, and training and capacity development activities to be implemented in partnership with the FIATA and CFCFA;
(iv)   implementation of advance shipping notification, paired with robust risk management systems, to help expedite cargo clearance in sea ports and dry ports;
(v)   deployment of common data interchange standards and advanced information systems to enable smooth electronic data interchange among CAREC member countries' shippers, carriers, and border management authorities; and
(vi)   support implementation of relevant international transport conventions and regional transport agreements to facilitate freedom of transit within CAREC internal waterways.

29.   Under the CTS 2030, modern ICT shall support seamless transport operations along the CAREC transport corridors. Relevant ICT

components will be integrated in CAREC transport projects to enhance cross-border transport time and cost. The most relevant ICT-related project components include:

(i)   security equipment and business process streamlining at land border crossing points and sea ports;

(ii) Intelligent Transport Systems to enable efficient management of traffic in congested areas near sea ports, at border crossing points, in urban areas, and in severe weather-impacted areas, such as mountain regions;

(iii) combining transport infrastructure development with high-performance communication lines, where practical; and

(iv) trade and general governance information systems, such as National Single Windows for Trade, that may have a positive impact on international trade cost and time.

30.   The private sector will be engaged for the development of smooth cross-border transport operations. With support of the CFCFA, the CAREC program will continue to monitor speed and cost of travel along the CAREC transport corridors by rail and road. Deeper engagement of the CFCFA will help provide in-depth analysis of transport and logistics issues along the CAREC corridors, contribute to recommendations to reduce time and cost of cross-border transport, and support the implementation of priority actions.

31.   The CAREC program will prioritize the holistic improvement of the business logistics environment to enable seamless end-to-end trade and transport within the CAREC region and beyond. The CAREC program will strive to improve logistics performance of all DMCs along all pillars monitored by the Logistics Performance Index.[10] Training and capacity development in logistics and supply chain management in CAREC DMCs will be crucial for a long-term improvement in regional logistics performance.

---

[10]   World Bank. 2018. Logistics Performance Index. https://lpi.worldbank.org/international/global.

CHAPTER V

Strategic Pillar—Roads and Road Asset Management

32. **CAREC and Roads and Road Asset Management (RAM).** Over the last decade, investments in the road sector focused on the construction and rehabilitation of priority road networks in CAREC countries to increase the standard and condition of these roads to meet current and future transport needs. To ensure the long-term sustainability of these road improvements, the TTFS 2020 envisaged the development of Road Asset Management Systems (RAMS) and the implementation of performance-based maintenance (PBM) contracts in several CAREC DMCs. To support this objective, a regional Road Asset Management Workshop was held in April 2015, followed by the preparation and dissemination of three road asset management publications. DMCs designed and used CAREC self-assessment tools to assess their status and capacity to implement robust RAMS. Throughout the TTFS 2020 implementation period, the CAREC DMCs and development partners continued working on the modality of PBM contracts and arrangements for development financing of the PBM-related projects.

33. **Key issues.** Despite improvements of the CAREC road network infrastructure and road maintenance practices, budgets prioritize construction and rehabilitation and the existing funding allocation for maintenance only covers a fraction of the estimated need. Furthermore, the limited maintenance funding is not necessarily needs- and demand-driven, but tends to be targeted at older roads in poor condition. As a result, proper maintenance of recently completed road networks is lacking in most CAREC DMCs. This led to accelerated deterioration of these roads which reduced the actualization of travel time savings expected from the investments.[11] Moreover, a lack of investment in upfront, routine, and preventive maintenance reduces the life span of the assets, as the roads will get to a point where they are no longer maintainable, requiring costly rehabilitation or reconstruction. As a result, countries have been unconsciously increasing life cycle costs of the road assets.

34. **Actions.** The objective of this strategic pillar of the CAREC program is to strengthen road asset management in the CAREC countries to respond to these issues. Road asset management is a strategic approach that seeks the optimal allocation of resources for the management, operation, preservation, and enhancement of road infrastructure to meet the needs of current and future road users. Road asset management looks at the optimization of available funding and determines the optimal allocation of this funding to different roads and investment types, with the aim of maximizing the benefits of improved road conditions and reduced road user costs over time. By collecting and analyzing data regarding the road network and its users, governments can make more informed choices regarding the allocation of

---

[11] Although road deterioration negatively impacts travel times, an even more significant cause of delays is related to border crossings.

funding to either develop, rehabilitate, or maintain an ever-expanding network of roads. This may also consider any expected climate change impacts. This approach introduces a shift in focus from short-term targets regarding the upgrading of road standards, to the long-term benefits of road maintenance for asset sustainability and future road sector funding requirements.

35.   Although CAREC supports the ongoing general development of six CAREC road corridors, the emphasis of future investment and technical assistance will increasingly be on routine and periodic maintenance[12] of completed roads through to 2030. This will be combined with the introduction and further development of RAMS that optimize and categorize the allocation of maintenance funding in relation to long-term road conditions and costs.

36.   The RAMS approach focuses on optimizing the efficiency and effectiveness of funding allocations in the road sector. The RAMS allows governments to predict future conditions of the road network and determine the impact that different funding levels and allocation will have on the road network in the long term. Optimization of funding levels and allocation generally results in a shift in focus from capital investment toward preservation of roads in good or fair condition, giving priority to roads with higher traffic volumes. By 2019, Pakistan was the only CAREC country with a fully mainstreamed and integrated RAMS for its national highway network, although several other member countries also progressed in this direction. In Pakistan, the RAMS resulted in a shift in funding allocation from rehabilitation to periodic maintenance, and a significant reduction in the average roughness of its highway network.

Box: Road Asset Management System Analysis at Different Budget Levels

The example below shows a road asset management system analysis depicting the expected highway conditions over time for Yunnan Province in the People's Republic of China based on different budget levels and allocation strategies. The first graph is based on current budget levels where allocations focus on the rehabilitation of a limited number of roads in poor condition, leading to the gradual deterioration of the rest of the road network which does not receive funding. In the second graph, the allocation is optimized for the same budget, focusing on roads with high traffic volumes and prioritizing preventive maintenance of roads in good or fair condition. This allows a greater portion of the network to be maintained and results in overall better road conditions, especially for high volume roads (T4). The third graph shows how an increase in the budget allows a greater portion of the road network to be rehabilitated and maintained, with further improvement of the road conditions over time (again focusing on roads with higher traffic volumes).

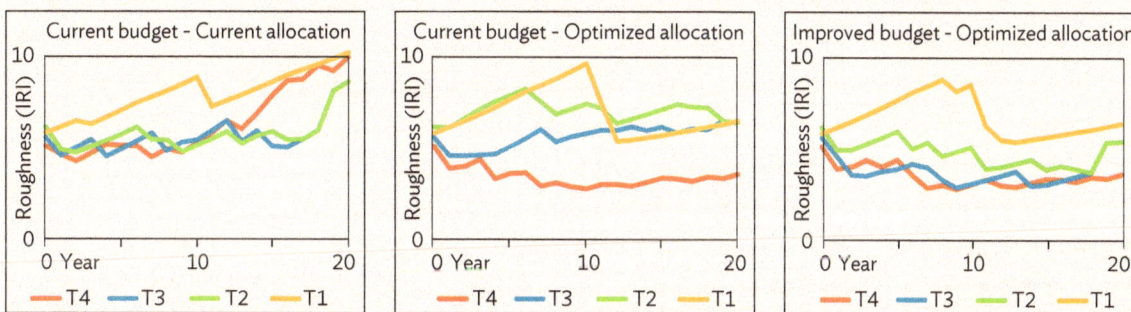

T1≤1000ADT, 1000ADT<T2≤2000ADT, 2000ADT<T3≤4000ADT, T4>4000ADT, ADT = average daily traffic, IRI = International Roughness Index.
Source: ADB. 2011. *Technical Assistance for Yunnan Sustainable Road Maintenance Project*. Manila.

---

[12]   Routine maintenance refers to activities carried out on a regular basis to ensure the proper functioning of road elements (e.g., clearing drains) and to carry out small repairs (e.g., patching potholes). Periodic maintenance refers to activities carried out every few years in a significant portion of the road to rejuvenate the pavement and other road elements.

Table 2: **Components of Road Asset Management**

RAMS = Road Asset Management System.
Source: CAREC Secretariat.

37.   However, a RAMS is only a tool and to function properly, it must be integrated within the wider road asset management context, including financing mechanisms, planning procedures, implementation modalities, and the institutional framework (Table 2). This integration tends to be the main barrier for countries to achieve the full benefit of a RAMS. Therefore, the CAREC program will pay significant attention to working with member countries to ensure their RAMS link up properly with existing road management procedures, or assist in the adjustment of these procedures, where necessary and desirable.

38.   This will involve looking at possible financing mechanisms and different funding levels for road maintenance, developing strategies to ensure adequate funding for maintenance operations and predicting the impact on future road conditions and road user costs. Special attention will be given to the introduction and development of road user charges as a source of maintenance funding. The CAREC program will furthermore determine how RAMS may support existing planning procedures in CAREC countries, strengthening decision making based on objective data analysis. The need for institutional reforms will be assessed, ensuring the required institutional capacities exist to run the RAMS and to implement the resulting plans. Alternative implementation modalities will be reviewed to identify options that provide suitable incentives for the timely execution of road maintenance in line with plans.

> Different financing mechanisms are used in the CAREC member countries. For road network development, general budget allocations and donor funding are commonly used. Although general budget allocations are also common for financing road maintenance, there is a growing tendency to introduce earmarked road user charges. Common road user charges include fuel taxes, vehicle registration fees, heavy vehicle surcharges, and tolls.

39.   In support of road asset management, the CAREC program will also assist the further introduction of performance-based maintenance contracts (PBM).[13] PBM facilitate the management of road maintenance and improve predictability of the resulting road conditions, while also increasing interest from contractors and providing incentives to invest in maintenance equipment and carry out repairs in a timely manner. As such, they complement RAMS very well. Mature experiences with PBM have resulted in cost savings of 15%–30% compared to traditional approaches (Table 3). The 14th Transport Sector Coordinating Committee (TSCC) Meeting in April 2015 confirmed region-wide interest in implementing PBM, and since then, several countries successfully piloted PBM maintenance programs, with plans for further expansion. The CAREC program will continue to support member countries in addressing the challenges faced in PBM, such as the use of suitable performance indicators and incentive structures, the lack of experience of the local contracting industry, and the effects of vehicle overloading on road conditions.

---

[13]   PBMs involve multiannual road maintenance contracts that require contractors to ensure that road conditions comply with predefined minimum performance standards at all times.

Table 3: Cost Savings of Performance-Based Contracts

Country	Reported Savings
Australia	10%–40%
Brazil	15%–35%
Canada	20%
Estonia	20%–40%
Finland	18%
The Netherlands	30%–40%
New Zealand	15%–38%
United States	10%–15%

Source: International Overview of Innovative Contracting Practices for Roads, 2007.

40.   CAREC will work with member countries to structure and implement RAMS and PBM to encourage appropriate road maintenance strategies in accordance with the conditions and characteristics of each member country. Effective implementation will require significant funding commitments from the public and private sectors, as well as the political will of transport and government agencies to undertake institutional and regulatory reforms. It will also require active participation of the private sector in both works implementation and management support.

41.   CAREC will serve as a leading platform for knowledge dissemination and regional workshops in the application of RAMS and PBM. In 2018, the CAREC Secretariat produced a compendium identifying 11 best practices crucial to the successful introduction and integration of RAMS.[14] In the same year, a guide on performance-based road maintenance contracts was also prepared, identifying best practices and lessons learned from various countries.[15] These two documents form the basis for the further introduction and development of RAMS and PBM in CAREC member countries. The CAREC program will also provide wider support for the improvement of road asset management in the member countries, ensuring financing mechanisms, planning procedures, institutional frameworks, and implementation modalities allow the RAMS and PBM to be used to their full potential.

42.   CAREC will provide a platform to help facilitate dialogue between different government agencies, and between different countries, which is crucial given the need for collaboration across multiple agencies to effectively implement road maintenance. Due to the huge regional variance in approaches to road maintenance, member countries will benefit from the sharing of best practice knowledge that CAREC provides.

---

[14]   ADB. 2018. *Compendium of Best Practices in Road Asset Management.* Manila. https://www.adb.org/publications/compendium-best-practices-road-asset-management.

[15]   ADB. 2018. *Guide to Performance-based Road Maintenance Contracts.* Manila.https://www.adb.org/documents/guide-performance-based-road-maintenance-contracts.

CHAPTER VI

Strategic Pillar—Road Safety

43. CAREC and road safety. Road crashes are the eighth leading cause of death globally and the sixth in Central Asia as of 2014. Improvements in road safety can dramatically reduce deaths and injuries while delivering significant social and economic benefits. For example, in Western Europe, where serious efforts have been made to improve road safety, road crashes are the 24th leading cause of death.[16] Thus, road crashes are preventable through adoption of internationally accepted road safety practices based on sound research.

44. Key issues. While road traffic death rates decreased by about 15% on average since 2010 across all CAREC countries, the number of annual road traffic fatalities (60,000) and injuries (600,000) remain high in the CAREC region (Figure 3).[17] As of 2018, the road traffic death rates range from 8.7 to 18.1 per 100,000 population across CAREC countries as compared to 2.8 in Sweden and 3.1 in the United Kingdom.[18] Road traffic fatalities are just the tip of the iceberg. For every reported death, a number of people are injured which has drastic consequence for the individuals involved and their families, such as permanent disabilities.

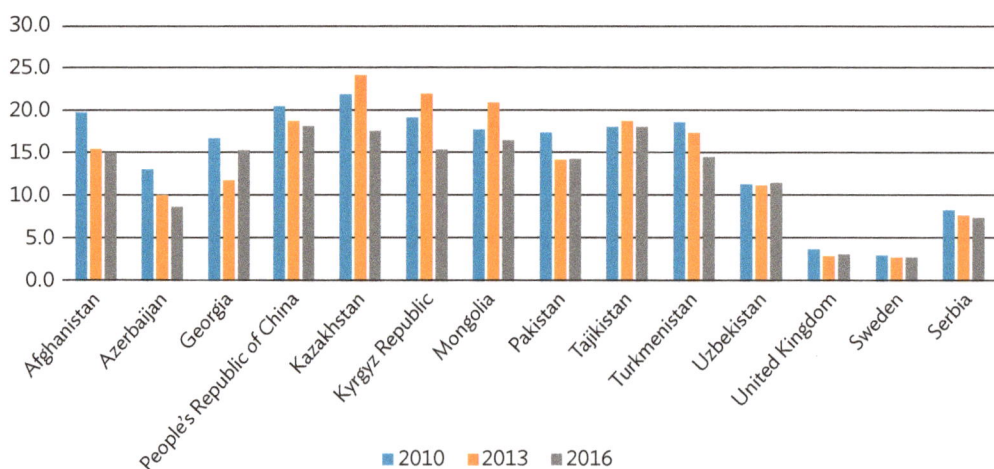

Figure 3: Estimated Road Traffic Death Rates in CAREC Countries, Serbia, Sweden, and the United Kingdom, 2010, 2013, and 2016
(per 100,000 population)

Source: World Health Organization.

---

[16] Global Road Safety Facility, The World Bank; Institute for Heath Metrics and Evaluation. 2014. *Transport for Heath: The Global Burden of Disease from Motorized Road Transport.* Seattle (IHME) and Washington (World Bank).

[17] A road traffic fatality is defined as a death occurring within 30 days of a road traffic crash.

[18] World Health Organization. 2018. *Global Status Report on Road Safety.* Geneva.

45.   Road safety legislation, design standards, and practices in many countries do not reflect international good practice. Collection, reporting, and sharing of data on road crashes and casualties is limited in many member countries, thereby restricting the ability to formulate informed road safety action plans. Furthermore, both requisite skills and knowledge of good practice relating to road safety are limited throughout the region. This includes critical areas, such as performing road safety audits, black-spot investigations, effective road policing, road safety education and awareness campaigns, and first aid services provided by first responders. Long-term commitment from CAREC member countries is essential for safer roads. It is also essential to continuously update road safety regulations to be aligned with international good practices.

46.   **Actions.** Following the 14th CAREC Ministerial Conference in September 2015, the CAREC Road Safety Working Group was first established. This subsequently led to the preparation of the CAREC Road Safety Strategy 2017–2030 approved in 2016.[19] The CAREC Road Safety Strategy endorsed a reference framework to guide and implement all future road safety-related activities, which is directly aligned with the United Nations' Decade of Action for Road Safety 2011–2020 and Sustainable Development Goals (SDGs).[20]

47.   The CAREC Road Safety Strategy's vision statement is to "make CAREC international road corridors safe, efficient, and attractive for all road users." The CAREC Road Safety Strategy aims to reduce the number of global deaths and injuries from road crashes by 50% by 2030, relative to 2010 levels. In the CAREC context, this would result in at least 23,000 lives saved and 250,000 injuries avoided each year. The CAREC Road Safety Strategy includes a number of specific output indicators and targets.

48.   Following approval of the CAREC Road Safety Strategy, promising progress was made in mainstreaming and integrating road safety engineering in the design and implementation of CAREC road projects. The vast majority of CAREC road projects are subject to road safety audits before and during construction. A series of three road safety manuals (road safety audit, safer road works, and roadside hazard management) were developed and disseminated through national training workshops to support and guide DMCs' efforts.

49.   CAREC countries will continue implementing the CAREC Road Safety Strategy in the period up to 2030. Implementation efforts will focus to a greater extent on road safety management (pillar 1) and safer road infrastructure (pillar 2), which involve direct collaboration with transport ministries in member countries. Safer road vehicles (pillar 3), safer roads users (pillar 4), and emergency post-crash care (pillar 5) will also receive due attention in line with each country's needs and priorities (Figure 4).

50.   Priority actions under pillars 1 and 2 may include (i) developing national road safety strategies and action plans, (ii) improving collection and monitoring of crash data, (iii) upgrading road design standards, (iv) institutionalizing road safety audits processes, (v) eliminating hazardous locations on existing road networks, (vi) developing road safety engineering capacities, and (vii) improving safety at road work sites.

---

[19]   ADB. 2016. *Safely Connected: A Regional Road Safety Strategy for CAREC Countries (2017–2030)*. Manila.
[20]   Two of the SDGs' targets are specifically related to road safety: target 3.6 aims to halve the number of global deaths and injuries from road traffic accidents by 2020, and target 11.2 seeks to provide access to sustainable and safe transport systems.

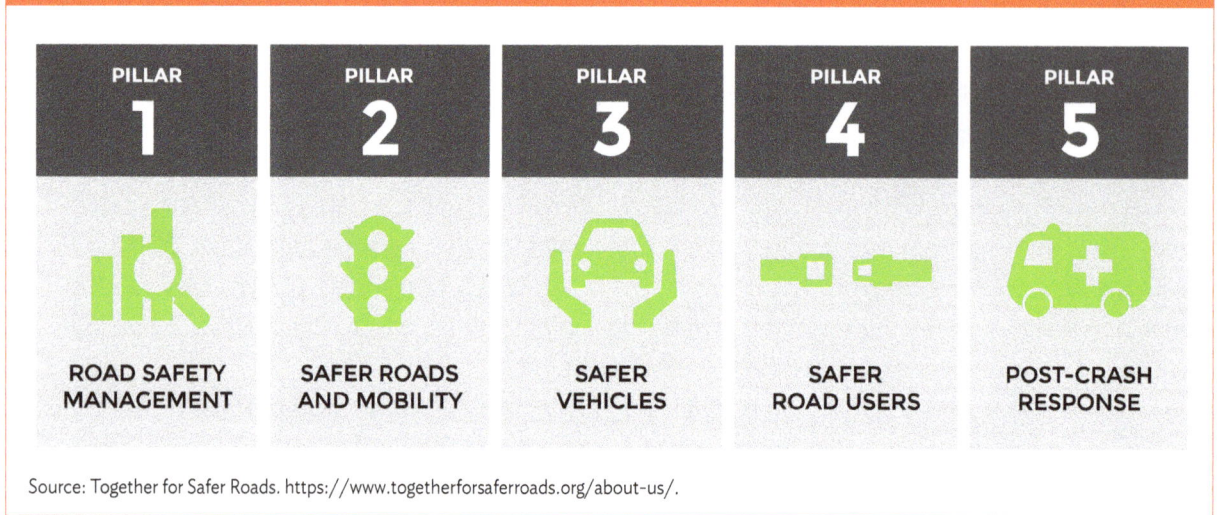

Figure 4: Five Pillars of the United Nations Decade of Action for Road Safety

PILLAR 1	PILLAR 2	PILLAR 3	PILLAR 4	PILLAR 5
ROAD SAFETY MANAGEMENT	SAFER ROADS AND MOBILITY	SAFER VEHICLES	SAFER ROAD USERS	POST-CRASH RESPONSE

Source: Together for Safer Roads. https://www.togetherforsaferroads.org/about-us/.

51.   Overall, the CAREC program will help catalyze priority road safety actions through (i) project preparation, (ii) peer learning, (iii) knowledge sharing, (iv) capacity development, (v) policy dialogue, and (vi) technical assistance and investment financing. Use of high-level technologies and preparation and implementation of full-fledged road safety programs through alternative financing modalities (e.g., results-based or policy-based lending) will be given special attention.

52.   To better facilitate coordination of each country's road safety initiatives, which typically involve several stakeholders, the CAREC TSCC will provide a platform to monitor progress and facilitate experience sharing across member countries. Ad hoc regional and national meetings will be regularly held to advance the road safety agenda and help reinforce a collective approach to achieving the targets of the CAREC Road Safety Strategy.

CHAPTER VII

Strategic Pillar—Railways

53. **CAREC and Railways.** Cognizant of the centrality of railway transport for enhancing multimodal connectivity, TTFS 2020 introduced the designated rail corridors concept to create conditions for seamless, uninterrupted train services across borders (Map 2). Railways are crucial to promoting economic diversification through the development of logistics and manufacturing supply chains. The efficient use of railways can also help countries to meet sustainable development goals on climate change, since they are generally a carbon-efficient mode of transport on a ton-kilometer or passenger-kilometer basis.[21] Railways are also characterized by their long economic life: movement of certain goods by rail—especially bulky and heavy goods—is cost-effective on routes which have been in existence for a long time and where capital expenditures have been amortized.

54. **Key issues.** Despite being geographically well-positioned to capture growing demand for transcontinental cargo traffic, the railway sector's share of CAREC regional cargo trade stagnated in favor of road transport. Underlying this trend is that consumer and market requirements are rapidly changing in favor of faster, cheaper, and user-friendly transport services. Railways need to improve the overall level of service to their clients and support the door-to-door movement of goods in tandem with other modes of transport to meet such requirements.

55. **Actions.** The CAREC Railway Working Group was established in April 2015 to offer a mechanism for CAREC countries to enhance regional cooperation in railways. The working group was tasked with formulating a strategy for rail to become a "transport mode of choice" by 2030. The strategy was completed in October 2016, and its framework is in Figure 5. The strategy highlights a comprehensive set of actions to be undertaken under a two-pronged approach to enhance the sector's performance, through improvements of physical infrastructure, as well as policies related to sector reform and commercialization. In support of these two approaches, the strategy sets out priorities in the areas of (i) development of effective rail infrastructure, (ii) development of robust commercial capabilities, and (iii) improvement of legal and regulatory frameworks. Targets are set for new railway construction and electrification, accompanied by measures to improve cost efficiency of rail freight.

56. In the period up to 2030, CAREC countries will work to implement the CAREC Railway Strategy. CAREC countries will use the Railway Working Group and its meetings to (i) deepen subsector assessments, (ii) develop and maintain a regional traffic model to support evidence-based planning of investments, (iii) conduct project preparation (screening, pre-feasibility), (iv) develop and disseminate knowledge, and (v) build the capacity of railway institutions.

---

[21] Intergovernmental Panel on Climate Change. 2018. *Fifth Assessment Report.* https://www.ipcc.ch/site/assets/uploads/2018/02/ipcc_wg3_ar5_chapter8.pdf.

Map 2: CAREC Designated Rail Corridors

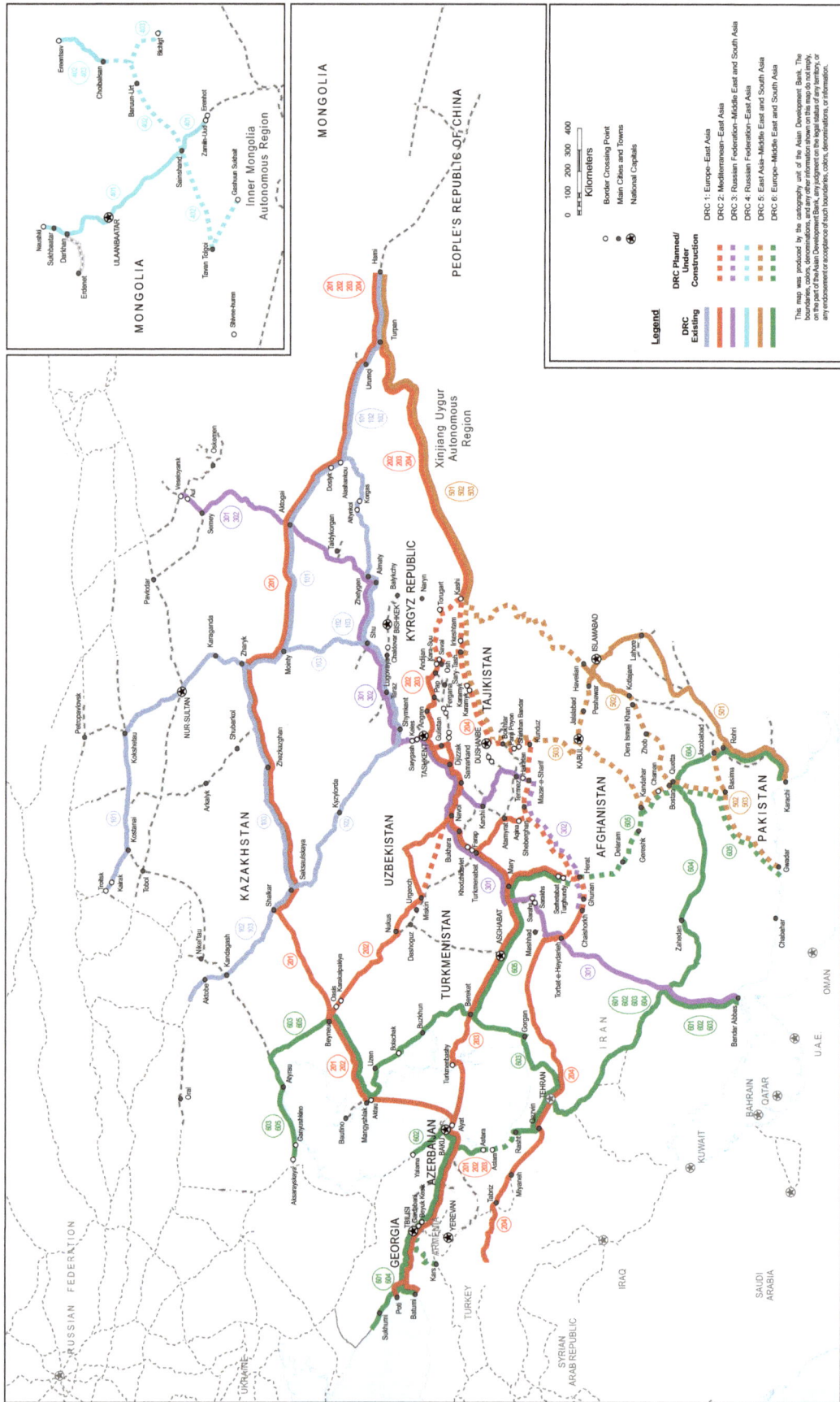

Legend

DRC
Existing

DRC Planned/
Under
Construction

DRC 1: Europe–East Asia
DRC 2: Mediterranean–East Asia
DRC 3: Russian Federation–Middle East and South Asia
DRC 4: Russian Federation–East Asia
DRC 5: East Asia–Middle East and South Asia
DRC 6: Europe–Middle East and South Asia

National Capitals
Main Cities and Towns
Border Crossing Point

Kilometers
0   100 200 300 400

This map was produced by the cartography unit of the Asian Development Bank. The
boundaries, colors, denominations, and any other information shown on this map do not imply,
on the part of the Asian Development Bank, any judgment on the legal status of any territory, or
any endorsement or acceptance of such boundaries, colors, denominations, or information.

RUSSIAN FEDERATION

MONGOLIA

Inner Mongolia
Autonomous Region

PEOPLE'S REPUBLIC OF CHINA

Xinjiang Uygur
Autonomous Region

KAZAKHSTAN

KYRGYZ REPUBLIC

UZBEKISTAN

TAJIKISTAN

TURKMENISTAN

AFGHANISTAN

PAKISTAN

ISLAMABAD

IRAN

TEHRAN

AZERBAIJAN

BAKU

ARMENIA

YEREVAN

GEORGIA

TBILISI

TURKEY

IRAQ

SYRIAN
ARAB REPUBLIC

SAUDI
ARABIA

KUWAIT

BAHRAIN

QATAR

U.A.E.

OMAN

UKRAINE

NUR-SULTAN

ASHGABAT

KABUL

DUSHANBE

BISHKEK

TASHKENT

MONGOLIA

ULAANBAATAR

DRC = designated rail corridors.
Source: CAREC Secretariat.

19-1649 AV

Figure 5: Framework of CAREC Railway Strategy

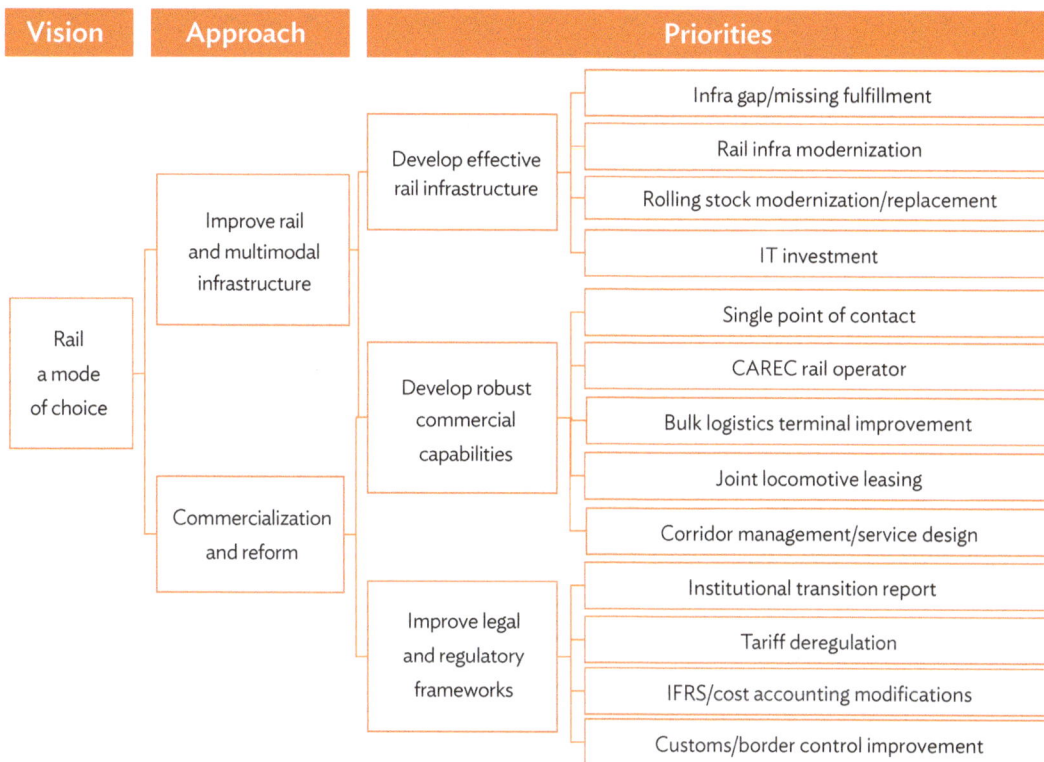

Vision	Approach	Priorities

Vision: Rail a mode of choice

Approach:
- Improve rail and multimodal infrastructure
- Commercialization and reform

Priorities:

Develop effective rail infrastructure
- Infra gap/missing fulfillment
- Rail infra modernization
- Rolling stock modernization/replacement
- IT investment

Develop robust commercial capabilities
- Single point of contact
- CAREC rail operator
- Bulk logistics terminal improvement
- Joint locomotive leasing
- Corridor management/service design

Improve legal and regulatory frameworks
- Institutional transition report
- Tariff deregulation
- IFRS/cost accounting modifications
- Customs/border control improvement

IFRS = International Financial Reporting Standards, IT = information technology.
Source: CAREC Secretariat.

57.   The Railway Working Group will undertake or update subsector assessments in each CAREC member country to enhance understanding among policy makers of the constraints facing each railway and solutions to overcome them.

58.   The Railway Working Group will develop and maintain an empirical model which CAREC member countries can use to forecast traffic, identify bottlenecks to further growth in traffic, and specify projects that can help to relieve such bottlenecks. Specific emphasis will be placed on border crossing points to determine the cause of delays at such locations and identify requisite solutions.

59.   The Railway Working Group will aim to formulate bankable investment projects and mobilize the large requisite resources by screening project options, performing prefeasibility studies, or validating existing prefeasibility studies. CAREC countries will work to prioritize railway projects that are economically and financially viable, significantly facilitate cross-border freight, encourage private sector participation, or complement wider institutional and regulatory reforms in individual countries. Important considerations will also be given to improve the environmental sustainability of railways, through modal shift, enhanced energy efficiency, and fuel switch (e.g., from diesel to electricity). Safety and security of railways will be pursued for rail service users (including specific solutions for women where applicable), railway workers, and the general public, for example, on matters relating to crashes at level crossings.

60.   To support the policy aspects of railway sector actions and outputs, the Railway Working Group will develop knowledge products and conduct events on topics prioritized by CAREC countries, such as state-owned enterprise reform, financial restructuring, asset management, tariff policies and regulation, border-crossing policies, interoperability, and environmental protection. The Railway Working Group will serve as a platform for providing training, capacity development, and introducing international best practice in these key areas. There will be heavy emphasis on regional knowledge sharing of such best practices. The platform will also help to facilitate better coordination between the different agencies responsible for railways in each country.

61.   The Railway Working Group will serve as a coordination mechanism among development partners to align their support to CAREC member countries. The Asian Development Bank (ADB) prepared a dedicated technical assistance project in response to the countries' requests in 2018 to support the initial implementation of the CAREC Railway Strategy in the aforementioned areas.[22] This will be combined and coordinated with other key initiatives of various CAREC development partners.

[22]   ADB. 2018. *Railway Sector Development in Central Asia Regional Economic Cooperation Countries.* Manila. https://www.adb.org/projects/52137-001/main.

CHAPTER VIII

Strategic Pillar—Aviation

62.   **CAREC and Aviation.** With much of the CAREC region being landlocked and facing physically restrictive geographies, air connectivity represents a vital transport option. Air connectivity is particularly key to moving perishable and high-value goods, as well as being a preferred option for time-constrained business travel and tourism. The strategic location of CAREC countries also implies the region holds the potential to be an aviation hub between Asia and Europe.

63.   Despite this significant potential, air connectivity between CAREC countries is quite sparse by international standards. As of September 2017, of the 55 country pairs within CAREC, only 26 were linked. In 2017, there were approximately 73,000 weekly seats between CAREC countries, including approximately 42,000 weekly seats between the PRC and other CAREC countries. CAREC countries are generally better linked to markets outside CAREC, with total weekly international capacity among the 10 CAREC countries to outside markets, excluding the PRC, reaching approximately 1 million seats in 2017. The PRC alone had more than 3.4 million international weekly seats.[23]

64.   Lack of competition and market access are the key factors inhibiting the sector's growth. The current scope of bilateral or multilateral air service agreements between countries remains extremely limited. Many CAREC airports also charge landing

fees, fuel prices, and higher taxes than the global average, while the regulatory environment in some countries encourages monopolistic practices by airlines.

65.   **Key issues.** CAREC initiated collaboration on the aviation sector with a study visit and training workshop in Singapore in April 2017. During this event, a consensus began to take shape that regional aviation connectivity was recognized as a core area for CAREC support. This finding was confirmed during the 2017 CAREC TSCC Meeting where it was decided to undertake a CAREC Scoping Study on Aviation. At this time, aviation was also formally recognized as the fifth pillar of the CAREC program. In September 2018, the CAREC Aviation Scoping Study was published and disseminated to member countries. It proposes a strategic framework for the Aviation pillar summarized in Figure 6.

66.   Given the relative unrealized potential of aviation for CAREC countries, addressing the following key issues would be pivotal in catalyzing greater regional air connectivity:

(i)   Phased approach to opening of air markets, including the initial permitting of "third" and "fourth" freedom rights for nondomestic airlines to serve intraregional routes.[24]

(ii)   Creation of an enabling environment for the introduction of low-cost carriers into

---

[23]   ADB. 2018. Aviation and the Role of CAREC: Scoping Study. Available at: https://www.adb.org/publications/aviation-role-carec-study.

[24]   ADB. 2018. Aviation and the Role of CAREC: Scoping Study. Available at: https://www.adb.org/publications/aviation-role-carec-study.

Figure 6: Framework of CAREC Aviation Pillar

Vision: Safe, reliable, and efficient aviation sector in the CAREC region.	
Priorities	**Areas for Intervention**
Policy and regulation	• Market development (phased approach) • Environmental policy and standards • Safety policy and standards
Infrastructure and equipment	• Airport facilities and equipment (terminals, runways, maintenance facilities) • Intermodality (connectivity to and from airports) • Fleet (aircraft ownership and procurement options) • Communications and navigation equipment, including equipment for managing overflights
Operations	• Airport operations (ownership and management, human resource capacity development) • Air navigation services providers (air navigation modernization plans, ownership, and management) • Air safety and security • E-cargo • Facilitation services (visa processes, customs, and others)

Source: ADB. 2018. *Aviation and the Role of CAREC: Scoping Study.* https://www.adb.org/publications/aviation-role-carec-study

---

the CAREC aviation market, particularly for underserved areas.

(iii) Strategic investment in aviation infrastructure, including airport upgrades and development in secondary cities with much tourism potential.

(iv) Upgrading of navigation and air safety equipment.

(v) Augmenting of fleets with new or leased aircraft, especially smaller aircraft for regional connectivity.

(vi) Provision of quality public transport and/or mass transport systems between cities centers and airports.

(vii) Strategic adoption of public–private partnership (PPP) models, when appropriate, to improve efficiencies of airport management, including catering services, retailing, parking, and duty-free concessions.

(viii) Policy and project commitment to the adoption of paperless e-cargo systems that allows the seamless movement of air cargo across the CAREC region.

(ix) Evaluation of visa policies and aviation fee structures to better permit the free flow of passengers and freight through the region, as well as the encouragement of a joint tourism strategy.

67.   **Actions.** CAREC partners are well-placed to facilitate a move toward a more open and effective aviation market across the region. The CAREC program provides a platform to promote bilateral and multilateral air service agreements, along with other forms of regional modernization of the aviation sector. CAREC could play a role with technical assistance to promote regulatory convergence and regional harmonization of common standards between member countries in areas including airspace management, transit agreements, navigation systems, and visa policies. This technical assistance could also be applied through consulting and knowledge services on critical industry issues, such as pre-feasibility and feasibility studies, gap analyses, regulatory reforms, managing infrastructure monopolies, and creating a supporting environment for PPPs.

68.   CAREC is likewise well-placed to provide capacity development and training support to member countries on aviation best practices. The initial CAREC aviation workshop was well-received and, from survey work under the CAREC Aviation Scoping Study, member countries expressed particular interest in further capacity development activities on regulations and policies (including open sky agreements) and airport management practices. The participation to date in CAREC capacity development by key international aviation organizations, including the International Civil Aviation Organization and the International Air Transport Association, should be encouraged to continue.

69.   CAREC partners are poised to offer finance and grant support to member countries for aviation initiatives, particularly efforts that can overcome obstacles to aviation's role in economic development. Private investment through PPP structures are viable in air transport, especially where there is sufficient passenger or cargo demand. In other instances, conditions may require partial or full public investment, especially in the case of secondary cities or isolated portions of a country, where air transport investment can be key to local economic development.

CHAPTER IX

Implementation Arrangements and Action Plan

70. The CAREC program is the joint-cooperation platform of 11 DMCs and international and bilateral development partners, with shared responsibility for choosing directions and priority actions. In 2000, ADB established the CAREC Secretariat to support primary CAREC activities. The core team of the CAREC Secretariat is based in Manila, with additional consultants based in CAREC countries. Every CAREC member country nominates CAREC national focal points, who are usually senior government officials of ministries of economy or finance; and sector focal points who represent relevant ministries or agencies, such as transport, energy, customs, and trade. Every year, the CAREC program holds several high-level regional events, such as the CAREC Ministerial Conference, Senior Officials Meeting (SOM), Sector Coordination Committees, and topical workshops and forums on transport, energy, customs, and trade.

71. The CAREC Transport Sector Coordination Committee (TSCC) will continue to be held annually, normally in the first half of the year or as agreed by CAREC countries, preceding the midyear CAREC SOM. The CAREC TSCC serves as a communication and coordination platform for DMCs and development partners to discuss key trends and priorities in global and regional transport, share experiences, present new projects and initiatives, and discuss action plans for short- and midterm horizons. Although most projects presented and discussed in the CAREC TSCC are

centered around the six CAREC transport corridors, they are also highly relevant to the broader CAREC network and transportation systems of the CAREC neighboring countries.

72. Regional Working Groups on railways, cross-border transport, road safety, road asset management, and other priority topics will be held annually, preferably back-to-back with the CAREC TSCC. The CAREC Secretariat will hold national training and capacity development workshops to improve capacity development and implementation of priority transport actions in individual countries. DMCs will be invited to express their interest in such national events based on their specific needs. In designing and implementing the national workshops, key attention will be given to opportunities for cross-country knowledge sharing.

73. One of the key success factors of the CAREC program is its strong focus on development and financing of transport infrastructure. The program will continue further development of CAREC transport infrastructure through identification and prioritization of projects which meet the objectives of regional connectivity and economic, social and ecological sustainability (Appendix 2). Communications and prefeasibility assessment support will be provided by the CAREC Secretariat to those projects which involve two or more countries and where coordination among the CAREC DMCs and development partners is required. Through the CAREC platform, co-

financing opportunities including private sector financing and PPP opportunities will be identified.

74.   In addition to establishing the platform for coordination and communication among the CAREC DMCs and development partners (DPs), the CAREC program will continue to prioritize the preparation and dissemination of knowledge products in relevant subsectors of transport. More attention will be given to knowledge products that support decision-making process of DMCs on specific transport-related policy reforms. Knowledge products will mostly be targeted at government policy decision makers, rather than technical transport experts.

75.   The CAREC Transport Sector's work will be led by the National Transport Sector Focal (NTSF) officials appointed by all DMCs. Through their appointed NTSF, DMCs will contribute to prioritization of actions under the CAREC transport agenda. The CAREC DMCs make all decisions under the CAREC transport agenda by consensus. CAREC transport DPs will also appoint focal points to represent their respective organizations.

76.   The CAREC Transport Secretariat (CAREC Secretariat) is established in ADB and includes ADB transport specialists, coordinators, and consultants. The CAREC Secretariat's coordinators and consultants are financed through technical assistance projects which in the past have been supported by ADB and other funding resources. Staff of other development partners, including but not limited to the World Bank, European Bank for Reconstruction and Development, Islamic Development Bank, International Road Transport Union, United Nations Economic and Social Commission for Asia and the Pacific, United Nations Economic Commission for Europe, and the Transport Corridor Europe–Caucasus–Asia will continue to provide technical, financial, and organizational support to the program.

77.   The CAREC Institute will upscale and align its transport-related knowledge generation, knowledge services, and knowledge management activities with this strategy. The CAREC Institute will continue providing strategic support by designing and delivering road safety and road asset management workshops in the CAREC countries, as well as further developing analytical and knowledge dissemination activities in the CAREC region's transport sector.

78.   The CAREC Transport Sector will increase engagement with private sector organizations of the DMCs, mostly transport and freight forwarding associations. The private sector organizations will provide independent monitoring data, consulting, and knowledge dissemination support. Knowledge products will be prepared to support development of the private sector in the CAREC region.

79.   The CAREC program will support improvement of connectivity between the CAREC DMCs and with the rest of the world, and of the sustainability of CAREC transport systems and networks. Key outcomes will be measured through travel time and cost of travel along CAREC transport corridors. Various outputs of the CAREC program will be measured to provide reference information for DMC and DP decision makers. The CAREC Secretariat will compile and report required information, and will conduct dedicated studies and analyses in cases where information is not readily available.

80.   The CAREC Transport Strategy 2030 will be monitored via the annual CAREC Transport Sector Progress Report and Rolling Action Plan, the outline content of which is in Table 4. Full use will be made of Corridor Performance Measurement and Monitoring (CPMM) and other indicators, with information updated and provided by individual countries and then consolidated into annual progress reports. Reviews of the CAREC Transport Strategy 2030 progress toward high-level outcomes

Table 4: CAREC Transport Sector Progress Report and Rolling Action Plan

Section	Key content	Data sources
Report on CAREC Transport work plan implementation	• CAREC Transport Sector completed stock-take of activities and lessons learned • Coordination Committees, Working Groups, training activities • Knowledge products completed, reports, publications	CAREC Secretariat
Transport projects update	• List of priority CAREC projects by country and corridor with latest updates	DMCs
Project achievements	• Summary of projects and initiatives that successfully integrated key topics of the Strategy	CAREC Secretariat, DMCs, DPs
Outcome level achievements	• Outcome indicators by pillar • Analytical reports, interpretation of data, lessons learned • Additional reports can be prepared as attachments to the Transport Sector Progress Report and Rolling Action Plan or stand-alone documents	All relevant per Appendix 3
Action plan for the next year	• Detailed action plan with specific activities listed: working groups, knowledge products, capacity development activities, and others • Will be approved by annual CAREC TSCC	CAREC Secretariat in consultation with DMCs and DPs
Indicative plan for the next 3 years	• Indicative priority activities for the next 3 years • Decisions on CAREC Transport Sector technical assistance resource requirements • Will be approved by annual CAREC TSCC	CAREC Secretariat in consultation with DMCs and DPs

CAREC = Central Asia Regional Economic Cooperation, DMC = developing member country, DP = development partner, TSCC = Transport Sector Coordinating Committee.
Source: CAREC Secretariat.

will take place annually during the meetings of sector professionals. Progress is unlikely to be uniform across all CAREC countries, and there should be adequate flexibility to accommodate potential future adjustments to objectives and the evolution of regional or individual country circumstances. As such, where possible, the indicators for the CAREC Transport Strategy 2030 High-Level Outcomes are expressed as movements on a spectrum, or refer to existing CAREC CPMM indicators. High-level indicators are drawn, where possible, from the associated subsector strategies (Appendix 3).

81.   The CAREC Transport Strategy 2030 will be implemented in a phased approach, in line with the overarching CAREC Strategy 2030 and the associated Rolling Strategic Action Plan. Implementation will also be synchronized, to the extent possible, with the national development plans of member countries, as well as other CAREC-led regional initiatives, such as the CAREC Integrated Trade Agenda 2030 which stipulated objectives to increase regional trade and investment flows within CAREC by 2030.

82.   The CAREC Transport Sector will follow the principle "Think Regionally, Act Locally." The CAREC DMCs will be supported in cascading the CAREC Transport Strategy 2030 priorities down to their own national transport sector strategies and action plans. The strategic alignment of the national transport strategies and action plans with the regional priorities of the CAREC Transport Strategy will help the CAREC DMCs achieve stronger coordination in transport. The national transport strategies and plans will contain country-specific result monitoring frameworks, performance targets, implementation arrangements, and accountability mechanisms, which each CAREC DMC will set based on its national priorities and circumstances. The CAREC Secretariat will collect and summarize key priorities, performance targets, and achieved outputs by individual country and will help the CAREC DMCs share their plans and achievements with each other through the annual Transport Sector Progress Report and Rolling Action Plan. The CAREC Secretariat and development partners will provide technical support to DMCs that need assistance in developing their national transport strategies or action plans.

Appendixes

Appendix 1: CAREC Corridor Alignments

Table A1.1: **CAREC Corridor 1: Europe–East Asia**

CAREC 1a		CAREC 1b		CAREC 1c	
Country/Route		**Country/Route**		**Country/Route**	
PRC	Hami	PRC	Hami	PRC	Hami
	Turpan		Turpan		Turpan
	Urumqi		Urumqi		Kashi
	Kuytun		Kuytun		Torugart/Topa (road) - BCP
	Jinghe		Jinghe	KGZ	Torugart - BCP
	Alashankou (rail and road) - BCP		Khorgos (road) - BCP		Naryn
KAZ	Dostyk (rail and road) - BCP	KAZ	Korgas (road) - BCP/LC		Balykchy
	Aktogay		Almaty		Kochkor
	Mointy		Merke - BCP (rail)		Jalal-Abad
	Karaganda		Taraz		Bishkek
	Nur-Sultan		Shymkent		Chaldovar - BCP (road/rail)
	Kostanai		Kyzylorda	KAZ	Merke - BCP (rail)
	Kairak (rail and road) - BCP		Aktobe		Sypatai Batyr (road)
RUS	Troitsk (rail and road) - BCP		Zhaisan (rail and road) - BCP		Shu
		RUS	Kos Aral (rail)		Mointy
			(Sagarchi) (road) - BCP		Zharyk
			Novomarkovka		Karaganda
					Nur-Sultan
					Kostanai
					Kairak (rail and road) - BCP
				RUS	Troitsk (rail and road) - BCP

BCP = border crossing point, CAREC = Central Asia Regional Economic Cooperation, KAZ = Kazakhstan, KGZ = Kyrgyz Republic, LC = Logistics Center, PRC = People's Republic of China, RUS = Russian Federation.

Source: CAREC Secretariat.

Table A1.2: CAREC Corridor 2: Europe–Mediterranean–East Asia

CAREC 2a

Country	Route
PRC	Hami
	Turpan
	Kashi
	Yierkeshitan (road) - BCP
KGZ	Irkeshtam (road) - BCP
	Sary-Tash
	Osh - LC
UZB	Kara-Suu (rail/road)
	Kara-Suu/Savay (rail/road)
	Andijan (split)
	Kokland - BCP
TAJ	Kanibadam (rail) - BCP
	Nau (rail) - BCP
	Bekabad (rail) - BCP
UZB	Djizzak (converge)
	Andijan (split)
	Angren - LC
	Tashkent
	Djizzak (converge)
	Samarkand
	Navoi (split)
	Bukhara
	Urgench (converge)
	Nukus
KAZ	Karakalpakstan (rail/road)
	Beyneu (rail)/Tazhen (road) - BCP
	Aktau - LC
AZE	Baku (port) - LC
	Yevlakh
	Agstafa
	Beyuk Kesik (rail) and Red Bridge (road) - BCP
GEO	Gardabani (rail) and Red Bridge (road) -BCP
	Tbilisi
	Kutaisi
	Senaki (split)
	Anaklia
	Poti
	Batumi
	Sarpi (road) - BCP
TUR	Sarp (road) - BCP

CAREC 2b

Country	Route
PRC	Hami
	Turpan
	Kashi
	Yierkeshitan (road) - BCP
KGZ	Irkeshtam (road) - BCP
	Sary-Tash
	Osh - LC
UZB	Kara-Suu (rail/road)
	Kara-Suu/Savay (rail/road)
	Andijan (split)
	Kokland - BCP
TAJ	Kanibadam (rail) - BCP
	Nau (rail) - BCP
	Bekabad (rail) - BCP
UZB	Djizzak (converge)
	Andijan (split)
	Angren - LC
	Tashkent
	Djizzak (converge)
	Samarkand
	Navoi (split)
	Bukhara
	Alat - BCP
	Farap - BCP
TKM	Mary
	Ashgabat
	Turkmenbashi - LC
AZE	Baku (port) - LC
	Alyat - LC
	Yevlakh
	Agstafa
	Beyuk Kesik (rail) and Red Bridge (road) - BCP
GEO	Gardabani (rail) and Red Bridge (road) - BCP
	Tbilisi
	Kutaisi
	Senaki (split)
	Anaklia
	Poti
	Batumi
	Sarpi (road) - BCP
TUR	Sarp (road) - BCP

CAREC 2c

Country	Route
PRC	Hami
	Turpan
	Urumqi
	Kuytun
	Jinghe
	Alashankou (rail and road) - BCP
KAZ	Dostyk (rail and road) - BCP
	Aktogay
	Mointy
	Zharyk
	Zhezkazghan
	Saksaulskaya
	Shalkar
	Beyneu (rail) Tazhen (road) - BCP
	Aktau - LC
AZE	Baku (port) - LC
	Yevlakh
	Agstafa
	Beyuk Kesik (rail) and Red Bridge (road) - BCP
GEO	Gabdabani (rail) and Red Bridge (road) - BCP
	Tbilisi
	Kutaisi
	Senaki (split)
	Anaklia
	Poti
	Batumi
	Sarpi (road) - BCP
TUR	Sarp (road) - BCP

CAREC 2d

Country	Route
PRC	Hami
	Turpan
	Kashi
	Yierkeshitan (road) - BCP
KGZ	Irkeshtam (road) - BCP
	Sary-Tash
	Karamyk - BCP
TAJ	Dushanbe
	Bokhtar
	Panji Poyon - LC/BCP
AFG	Shirkhan Bandar - BCP
	Kunduz
	Mazar-e-Sharif
	Andkhoy
	Aqina
	Farap (rail/road) - BCP
TKM	Mary
AFG	Herat

AFG = Afghanistan, AZE = Azerbaijan, BCP = border crossing point, CAREC = Central Asia Regional Economic Cooperation, GEO = Georgia, KAZ = Kazakhstan, KGZ = Kyrgyz Republic, LC = Logistics Center, PRC = People's Republic of China, TAJ = Tajikistan, TKM = Turkmenistan, TUR = Turkey, UZB = Uzbekistan.

Source: CAREC Secretariat.

Table A1.3: CAREC Corridor 3: Russian Federation–Middle East and South Asia

CAREC 3a		CAREC 3b	
Country/Route		**Country/Route**	
RUS	Rubtsovsk	RUS	Rubtsovsk
	Veseloyarsk (rail and road) – BCP		Veseloyarsk (rail and road) – BCP
KAZ	Aul (rail and road) – BCP	KAZ	Aul (rail and road) – BCP
	Semey		Semey
	Charskaya		Charskaya
	Aktogay		Aktogay
	Taldykorgan		Taldykorgan
	Kapchagay		Kapchagay
	Almaty		Almaty
	Merke – BCP		Merke – BCP
	Taraz	KGZ	Chaldovar (rail) – BCP
	Shymkent		Kara-Balta
	Saryagash/Yallama (rail) and Zhibek Zholy (road) – BCP		Bishkek
UZB	Keles (rail) and Gisht Kyprik (road) – BCP		Kordai
	Tashkent		Osh – LC
	Syrdaryinskaya		Sary-Tash
	Djissak		Karamyk (road) – BCP
	Samarkand	TAJ	Karamyk (road) – BCP
	Navoi		Dushanbe
	Bukhara		Tursunzade
	Alat (rail and road) – BCP		Pakhtaabad (rail and road) – BCP
TKM	Farap (rail and road) – BCP	UZB	Saryasia (rail and road) – BCP
	Mary		Termez/Airatom (rail and road) – BCP
	Sarahs	AFG	Hairatan (rail and road) – BCP
IRN	Sarakhs		Mazar-e-Sharif
			Andkhoy
			Herat
			Islam Qala (road) – BCP
		IRN	Dogharoun (road) – BCP

AFG = Afghanistan, BCP = border crossing point, CAREC = Central Asia Regional Economic Cooperation, IRN = Iran, KAZ = Kazakhstan, KGZ = Kyrgyz Republic, LC = Logistics Center, RUS = Russian Federation, TAJ = Tajikistan, TKM = Turkmenistan, UZB = Uzbekistan.

Source: CAREC Secretariat.

Table A1.4: **CAREC Corridor 4: Russian Federation–East Asia**

CAREC 4a		CAREC 4b		CAREC 4c	
Country/Route		Country/Route		Country/Route	
RUS	Tashanta (road) - BCP	RUS	Naushki - BCP	RUS	Naushki - BCP
MON	Ulaanbaishint/Tsagaanur (road) - BCP	MON	Sukhbaatar - BCP	MON	Sukhbaatar - BCP
	Olgii		Ulaanbaatar		Ulaanbaatar
	Khovd		Zamiin-Uud (rail/road) - BCP		Chinggis
	Yarant (road) - BCP	PRC	Erenhot (rail/road) - BCP		Baruun-Urt
	Takeshikent (road) - BCP				Bichigt - BCP
PRC	Urumqi				

BCP = border crossing point, CAREC = Central Asia Regional Economic Cooperation, MON = Mongolia, PRC = People's Republic of China, RUS = Russian Federation.

Source: CAREC Secretariat.

Table A1.5: CAREC Corridor 5: East Asia–Middle East and South Asia

CAREC 5a		CAREC 5b		CAREC 5c	
Country/Route		**Country/Route**		**Country/Route**	
PRC	Hami	PRC	Hami	PRC	Hami
	Turpan		Turpan		Turpan
	Kashi		Kashi		Kashi
	Yierkeshitan (road) – BCP		Mansehra		Yierkeshitan (road) – BCP
KGZ	Irkeshtam (road) – BCP		Havelian	KGZ	Irkeshtam (road) – BCP
	Sary-Tash		Hasanabdal		Sary-Tash
	Karamyk (road) – BCP		Islamabad		Karamyk (road) – BCP
TAJ	Karamyk (road) – BCP		Lahore	TAJ	Karamyk (road) – BCP
	Dushanbe		Pindi Bathian		Dushanbe
	Bokhtar		Faisalabad		Bokhtar
	Panji Poyon – LC/BCP	PAK	Gojra		Panji Poyon – LC/BCP
AFG	Shirkhan Bandar (road) – BCP		Shorkot	AFG	Shirkhan Bandar (road) – BCP
	Kunduz		Khanewal		Kunduz
	Kabul		Multan		Kabul
	Jalalabad		Muzaffargarh		Ghazni
	Tokham (road) – BCP		Dera Ghazi Khan		Qalat
PAK	Landi Kotal (road) – BCP		Ratodero		Kandahar
	Peshawar		Sehwan	PAK	Chaman
	Islamabad		Karachi		Quetta
	Lahore				Kalat
	Pindi Bathian				Surab
	Faisalabad				Basima
	Gojra				Hoshab
	Shorkot				Gwadar
	Khanewal				
	Multan				
	Muzaffargarh				
	Dera Ghazi Khan				
	Ratodero				
	Sehwan				
	Karachi				

AFG = Afghanistan, BCP = border crossing point, CAREC = Central Asia Regional Economic Cooperation, KGZ = Kyrgyz Republic, LC = Logistics Center, PAK = Pakistan, PRC = People's Republic of China, TAJ = Tajikistan.

Source: CAREC Secretariat.

Table A1.6: CAREC Corridor 6: Europe–Middle East and South Asia

CAREC 6a		CAREC 6b		CAREC 6c		CAREC 6d	
Country/Route		Country/Route		Country/Route		Country/Route	
RUS	Krasnyi Yar (road)/ Aksaraskaya (rail) - BCP	RUS	Orenburg	RUS	Orenburg	RUS	Krasnyi Yar (road)/ Aksaraskaya (rail) - BCP
	Kurmangazy (road)/ Ganyushkino(rail) - BCP		Novomarkovka (road)/ Kos Aral (rail) - BCP		Novomarkovka (road)/ Kos Aral (rail) - BCP		Kurmangazy (road)/ Ganyushking (rail) - BCP
KAZ	Makat		Zhaisan (road/rail) - BCP		Zhaisan (road/rail) - BCP	KAZ	Makat
	Beyneu (rail)/ Tazhen (road) - BCP		Aktobe		Aktobe		Beyneu
	Karapalkastan (road/rail) - BCP		Shalkar		Shalkar		Aktau
	Nukus	KAZ	Aral	KAZ	Aral		Bereket
	Urgench (split)		Kyzyl - Orda		Kyzyl - Orda	TKM	Ashgabat
	Turtkul		Shymkent		Shymkent		Mary
	Gazli		Saryagash/Yallama (rail) and Zhibek Zholy (road) - BCP		Saryagash/Yallama (rail) and Zhibek Zholy (road) - BCP	AFG	Herat
UZB	Bukhara (converge)		Keles (rail) and Gisht Kuprik (road) - BCP		Keles (rail) and Gisht Kuprik (road) - BCP		Islam Qala - BCP
	Uchkuduk		Tashkent (split)	UZB	Tashkent (split)	IRN	Dogharoun - BCP
	Navoi		Djizzak		Khavast - BCP	AFG	Kandahar
	Bukhara (converge)	UZB	Ayni		Istaravshan - BCP		Chaman - BCP
	Karshi		Samarkand (converge)		Ayni		Quetta
	Boysun		Karshi	TAJ	Dushanbe		Kalat
	Termez/Airatom (rail/ road) - BCP		Boysun		Bokhtar	PAK	Surab
	Hairatan		Termez/Airatom (rail/ road) - BCP		Panji Poyon (road) - LC/ BCP		Basima
	Mazar-i-Sharif		Hairatan (rail/road) - BCP		Shirkan Bandar - BCP		Hoshab
AFG	Andkhoy		Mazar-e-Sharif		Kunduz		Gwadar
	Herat	AFG	Andkhoy		Pul-e-Khumri		
	Kandahar		Herat	AFG	Salang		
	Chaman - BCP		Islam Qala - BCP		Kabul		
	Quetta	IRN	Dogharoun - BCP		Jalalabad		
	Kalat	AFG	Kandahar		Torkham (road) - BCP		
PAK	Surab		Chaman - BCP		Landi Kotal (road) - BCP		
	Basima		Quetta		Peshawar		
	Hoshab		Kalat		Islamabad		
	Gwadar	PAK	Surab		Pindi Bhattian		
			Basima		Lahore		
			Hoshab		Faisalabad		
			Gwadar	PAK	Gojra		
					Shorkot		
					Khanewal		
					Multan		
					Muzaffargarh		
					Dera Ghazi Khan		
					Ratodero		
					Sehwan		
					Karachi		

AFG = Afghanistan, BCP = border crossing point, CAREC = Central Asia Regional Economic Cooperation, IRN = Iran, KAZ = Kazakhstan, LC = Logistics Center, PAK = Pakistan, RUS = Russian Federation, TAJ = Tajikistan, TKM = Turkmenistan, UZB = Uzbekistan.

Source: CAREC Secretariat.

Appendix 2: CAREC Priority Investment Projects by Country

No.	Country	Subsector	Project Title	Indicative Cost ($ million)	Indicative Implementation Period
1	AFG	Road	Qaisar–Laman Section of the Ring Road	700.0	2018–2021
2	AFG	Road	East West Corridor	530.0	TBD
3	AFG	Road	Kabul Ring Road Project (118.7 km)	158.0	2017–2023
4	AFG	Road	Kabul–Jalalabad	180.0	2019–2022
5	AFG	Road	North–South Corridor: Kandahar to Mazar-i-Sharif	550.0	2019–2023
6	AFG	Road	Salang Tunnel	600	2021–2025
7	AFG	Railway	Mazar-i-Sharif–Faryab–Herat Kandahar–Quetta railway line (1,288 km)	3,335.0	TBD
8	AZE	Ports	Construction of Grain Terminal in Baku Port	22.5	2019–2020
9	AZE	Ports	Construction of TIR Parking Area at Baku Port	9.0	2020
10	GEO	Ports	Construction of Anaklia Deep Sea Port (Phase 1)	586.0	2017–2020
11	GEO	Logistics	Development of Tbilisi Logistics Center	95.4	2020–2025 (Stage 1) 2026–2031 (Stage 2)
12	GEO	Logistics	Development of Kutaisi Logistics Center	72.5	2021–2026 (Stage 1) 2027–2032 (Stage 2)
13	GEO	Road	Construction of Rustavi–Red Bridge Highway	170.0	2020–2022
14	GEO	Road	Construction of Tbilisi Bypass Section	300.0	2023–2025
15	GEO	Road	Construction of Shorapani–Argveta Section	315.0	2020–2022
16	GEO	Road	Construction of Batumi–Sarpi Section	130.0	2020–2023
17	GEO	Road	Construction of Bridge over River Rioni in Poti	21.0	2020–2022
18	GEO	Road	Construction of Samtredi–Zugdidi Bypass Road	250.0	2025–2029
19	GEO	Road	Construction of Access Road to Anaklia Deep Sea Port	45.0	2019–2020
20	KAZ	Road	Reconstruction of Atyrau–Astrakhan Road	373.0	2017–2021
21	KAZ	Road	Reconstruction of Balkhash–Burylbaital Road	557.0	2017–2021
22	KAZ	Road	Reconstruction of Taldykorgan–Kalbatau Road	690.0	2017–2021
23	KAZ	Road	Reconstruction of Kurty–Kapshagai Road	61.0	
24	KAZ	Road	Almaty Ring Road (BAKAD) PPP – 20-year concession	600.0	2019–2039
25	KGZ	Aviation	Expanding Air Traffic Control (ATC) Capacity Project	46.0	2019–2023
26	KGZ	Aviation	Single navigation field of the Fergana Valley (installation of VOR/ DME equipment at Batken airport)	1.0	2019–2023
27	KGZ	Aviation	Construction of a new ATC tower at the Osh airport	3.0	2019–2023
28	KGZ	Road	Alternative North–South Road (99 km), Aral–Kazarman section (km 195–291) and construction of two elevated bridges	298.7	2015–2021
29	KGZ	Road	Connecting Road between CAREC 1 and CAREC 3 Transport Corridors (km 89–159, Epkin-Bashkuugandy).	114.4	2018–2021
30	KGZ	Road	Connecting Road between CAREC 1 and 3 Transport Corridors, 70.1 km (Balykchy-Kochkor-Epkin)	90.8	2019–2023
31	KGZ	Road	Rehabilitation of Bishkek–Osh road (Bishkek-Kara-Balta section)	100.0	2018–2020

continued on next page

Table: continued

No.	Country	Subsector	Project Title	Indicative Cost ($ million)	Indicative Implementation Period
32	KGZ	Road	Rehabilitation of Bishkek-Osh road (Jalal-Abad-Madaniyat section)	60.0	2016-2020
33	KGZ	Railway	Construction of a railway line PRC-Kyrgyz Republic-Uzbekistan	4,800.0	TBD
34	MON	Railway	Freight Wagon Manufacturing Facility in Sainshand, Dorno Gobi Province	61.0	2020-2025
35	MON	Railway	New Railway Line in Southern Mongolia	5,000.0	2020
36	MON	Road	Regional Road Development and Maintenance Project Phase I and II (Reconstruction of Altanbulag-Ulaanbaatar-Zamyn Uud Road CAREC 4b)	120.0	2018-2021
37	MON	Road	Regional Road Development and Maintenance Project Phase III (Reconstruction of Altanbulag-Ulaanbaatar-Zamyn Uud Road CAREC 4b)	120.0	2021-2024
38	MON	Road	Western Regional Road Corridor Investment Program (Khovd-Ulgii-Ulaanbaishint Road CAREC 4a)	58.0	2015-2020
39	MON	Road	Construction of 272 km paved road Baruun-Urt-Bichigt (Corridor 4c)	120.0	2019-2022
40	MON	Road	Advanced and smart technologies (control on vehicle movement, weight, dimension, emission, traffic intensity, and emergency mobile network) on 997 km of Zamiin-Uud-Ulaanbaataar-Altanbulag Road	4.5	2020
41	MON	Road	Ulaanbaatar-Darkhan road widening (four-lane expansion)	192.0	2019
42	MON	Logistics	Logistics Centers in the provinces of Bayan-Ulgii, Khovd, Darkhan-Uul	150.0	2020-2026
43	MON	Aviation	Upgrade of Khovd airport in Khovd Province	150.0	2019-2022
44	MON	Aviation	Upgrade of Tsagaandeglii Airport in Uvs Province	20.0	2020-2025
45	PAK	Road	Construction of 4-Lane Highway Rajanpur-Dera Ghazi Khan	300.0	2028-2031
46	PAK	Road	Construction of Additional Tunnel at Kohat	80.0	2021-2024
47	PAK	Road	Rehabilitation of Missing Section of Dera Ismail Khan-Yarak, N-55	20.0	2022-2023
48	PAK	Logistics	Improvement of BCP Sust (Pakistan-PRC border)	TBD	2021-2022
49	TAJ	Road	Obigarm-Nurobod Road Project (km 72-158)	484.0	2019-2025
50	TAJ	Road	Rehabilitation of Guliston-Farkhar-Pyandj-Dusti Road	39.8	2022-2024
51	TAJ	Road	Rehabilitation of Dushanbe-Rudaki-Yavan-A. Jomi-Sarband Road	50.4	2023-2025
52	TAJ	Road	Rehabilitation of Kurbonshakhid-Temurmalik road	24.0	2020-2022
53	TAJ	Road	Rehabilitation of Kyzlkkala-Kabadiyan-Shakhrituz-Aivadj road	51.7	2023-2025
54	TAJ	Road	Construction of a bridge across the Kafernigan river at km 9.8 of Dushanbe-Rudaki road	4.3	2023-2025
55	TAJ	Road	Construction of a bridge across the Elok river at km 11 of Dushanbe-Rudaki road	1.1	2021-2022

continued on next page

Table: continued

No.	Country	Subsector	Project Title	Indicative Cost ($ million)	Indicative Implementation Period
56	TAJ	Road	Construction of Labi Djar–Kalaikhumb road	335.0	2023–2025
57	TAJ	Railway	Construction of Tajikistan–Afghanistan–Turkmenistan railway	237.8	2023–2025
58	TAJ	Road	Rehabilitation of Kangurt–Temurmalik road	16.0	2020–2022
59	TAJ	Road	Construction of additional anti-avalanche galleries along Dushanbe–Chanak road (5,665 m)	51.5	2022–2025
60	TAJ	Road	Construction of Muminabad–Childukhtaron Road	4.2	2023–2025
61	UZB	Road	Rehabilitation of Karshi–Shakhrisabz–Kitab road (77 km)	198.0	2016–2021
62	UZB	Road	Rehabilitation of the A-380 highway Guzar–Bukhara–Nukus–Beyneu (km 228–315 section)	170.0	2016–2020
63	UZB	Road	Bukhara Region Road Network Improvement Project (km 150–188, and km 208–228)	230.0	2020–2024
64	UZB	Road	Bukhara Region Road Network Improvement Project: M-37 Samarkand–Bukhara–Osh (km 261–277, and km 287–365)	113.8	2020–2024
65	UZB	Road	Rehabilitation of 35-km road Guzar–Chim–Kukdala, km 38–73 section	50.0	2011–2019
66	UZB	Road	Reconstruction of A-380 Guzar–Bukhara–Nukus–Beyneu Road between Kungrad and Daut-ata (section 964–1204 km)	230.0	2020–2022
67	UZB	Road	Reconstruction of A-380 Guzar–Bukhara–Nukus–Beyneu (section 581–698 km)	TBD	2020–2022
68	UZB	Road	Reconstruction of M-39 Almaty–Bishkek–Tashkent–Termez (section 1037–1081 km)	TBD	2020–2022
69	UZB	Road	Reconstruction of M-41 Bishkek–Dushanbe–Termez–Sariasiya customs post (section 1444–1618 km)	TBD	2020–2022
70	UZB	Road	Reconstruction of M-37 Samarkand–Bukhara–Ashkhabad Bukhara–Alat customs post (sections 152–212, 212–241, 287–311, and 346–363 km)	TBD	2020–2022
71	UZB	Road	Reconstruction of A-376 Kokand–Dzhizak (section 246–299 km)	TBD	2020–2022
72	UZB	Railway	Railway Efficiency Improvement Project	170.0	2019–2021
73	UZB	Railway	Bukhara–Miskin–Urgench–Khiva Railway Electrification Project	250.0	2020–2024
74	UZB	Railway	Electrification of Pap–Namangan–Andijan railway section	80.0	2019–2020
75	UZB	Railway	Construction of electrified Angren–Pap railway line, with electrification of Pap–Kokand–Andijan section, with additional financing of SCADA system	545.0	2013–2021
76	UZB	Railway	Electrification of section of the railway Kashkadarya–Bukhara with organization of high-speed passenger trains	160.0	2020–2024
77	UZB	Aviation	Acquisition of four new Boeing 787-8 aircrafts	317.5	2016–2020

AFG = Afghanistan, AZE = Azerbaijan, CAREC = Central Asia Regional Economic Cooperation, DME = distance measuring equipment, GEO = Georgia, KAZ = Kazakhstan, KGZ = Kyrgyz Republic, km = kilometer, MON = Mongolia, PAK = Pakistan, PPP = public–private partnership, PRC = People's Republic of China, SCADA = supervisory control and data acquisition, TAJ = Tajikistan, TBD = to be determined, UZB = Uzbekistan, VOR = Very High Frequency Omni-Directional Range.

Source: CAREC Secretariat based on submissions of countries and development partners as of 2 September 2019.

Appendix 3: Outcome Level Indicators for CAREC Transport Sector

Pillar	Title	Outcomes	Indicators (Sources or Reports)
1	**Transport and Logistics Facilitation**	Efficiency improvements in border crossing points (BCPs), customs clearance, immigration procedures and cross-border logistics.	• Average speed by corridors, speed with delay (SWD) • Time and cost to clear a border crossing point, by corridor, country and BCP • Logistics Perception Index (LPI)
2	**Roads and Road Asset Management**	Improvement on the CAREC Road Asset Management (RAM) maturity model*	• 2019 (provisional): All countries at level 1 except Pakistan at level 3, for National Highway network (CAREC Transport Sector Progress Report) • Average speed of traffic without delay (SWOD), by corridors (CAREC CPMM) • Perception of highway quality improved (World Economic Forum Global Competitiveness Index) for selected countries
3	**Road Safety**	Reduction in the number of road crash fatalities on CAREC international road corridors	• By 2030: 50% reduction from 2010 figure (82,000 fatalities).
4	**Railways**	Improved service level and operation efficiency of railways	• CPMM average commercial speed, by CAREC corridor, SWD and SWOD • Perception of railway quality improved (World Economic Forum Global Competitiveness Index for railways) for selected countries
5	**Aviation**	Creation of a more open aviation market that catalyzes enhanced exchange and trade outcomes	• Number of CAREC country pairs achieving unrestricted third- and fourth-freedom rights • Number of CAREC countries adopting paperless e-freight systems for aviation • Number of countries with e-visa systems

* RAMS maturity model (Phase 1 – RAMS at construction; Phase 2 – RAMS provides full inventory assessment, albeit it can be at the fixed time, not regularly updated, not used in full for decision making and financial planning; Phase 3 – continuous (periodic) monitoring of the road asset inventory, good cost models, cost/management accounting and planning, decisions and financial planning based on all well-known factors and clear performance targets).

CAREC = Central Asia Regional Economic Cooperation, CPMM = Corridor Performance Measurement and Monitoring.

Source: CAREC Secretariat.

www.ingramcontent.com/pod-product-compliance
Lightning Source LLC
Chambersburg PA
CBHW040147200326
41519CB00035B/7619